Happily Ever After

Happily Ever After

Joy Wilt

Word Books, Publisher
Waco, Texas

HAPPILY EVER AFTER

ISBN 0–87680–491–1

Library of Congress catalog card number: 76–48498

Cover design and illustrations by Christopher Todd Wilt and Lisa Renée Wilt.

Dedicated to:
Richard and Doris Berry (Dad and Mom)
who, because of their love
and dedication in raising me,
are the heroes
in my "real life" story

Contents

Preface

Once upon a time, a long time ago, there was a little girl. She was an ordinary girl with freckles on her nose and long, brown hair. Her favorite thing in the world was fairy tales —especially the ones that ended with, ". . . and they lived happily ever after." She wanted more than anything else to live happily ever after, just like all the characters in the fairy tales.

One of her favorite fairy tales was Snow White. "Snow White lived happily ever after because she was a princess," the little girl thought to herself. "If I could be a princess, I could live happily ever after, too." And so she began plotting in her mind how she could become a princess. It didn't take long for her to realize that becoming a *real* princess would be quite impossible because her father was not a king and her mother was not a queen. The only thing left for her was to marry a prince and the only one she knew of lived in England. England was much too far away for her to go. Besides, she was too young to get married and she wanted to live happily ever after "right now."

Frustrated about not being able to be a princess, she abandoned the "Snow White" fairy tale for "Jack In The Beanstalk." "Jack lived happily ever after because he retrieved the giant's fortune and became rich!" she thought to herself. "If I'm going to live happily ever after, I'll have to be rich!" She began doing odd jobs around the house to earn extra money. She even ran a lemonade stand on the weekends. But alas, after a few weeks of hard work, she was disappointed to find that the contents of her piggy bank only added up to $5.02—a far cry from the million dollars that she needed in order to be rich!

Sadly, she chose another fairy tale to become her favorite. This time it was Rumpelstiltskin. "Living happily ever after means having a troll make things 'all better' when something bad happens to you," she thought. For months, she waited for the troll to come and bail her out whenever something bad happened to her, but he never came.

Disillusioned with fairy tales in general, the little girl began to believe that living happily ever after was an impossibility.

Then one day it happened. The little girl grew older and began to read a different kind of story. The hero in the new story was a kind, gentle man. He was not a handsome prince, he was not rich, and he experienced all kinds of bad things. Yet, he seemed to be happy. "How could this be?" the little girl wondered.

She read the stories over and over again until one day she began to understand.

By this time, the little girl was a grown woman. She reflected back on all the books she had read. Although she enjoyed the fairy tales very much, she decided that there needed to be another book. A book about real life. The book would help parents teach their children that

- It is not *who* you are that makes you happy, it is what you do with who you are;
- It is not *what* you have that makes you happy, it is what you do with what you have;
- It is not *living a problem-free life* that makes you happy, it's learning how to cope with problems and turning them into something good.

The little girl became so excited about the fact that *everyone* could live happily ever after, no matter who they were, what they had, or what happened to them that *she* decided to write a book about it . . . and so she did.

JOY WILT

Acknowledgments

Once upon a time, not long ago . . .
. . . there lived a man named Bruce E. Wilt, a brilliant, wise, loving man who, because of his kindness, faithfulness, and dedication, typed and edited this entire book.

. . . there lived two children named Christopher Todd and Lisa Renée who graciously allowed their life experiences to be included in the contents of this book so that parents and children everywhere could learn and profit from them.

. . . there lived several wonderful people who have had a positive influence on my life and have also kindly consented to read and comment on the manuscript. They are (in alphabetical order):

Dorothy Arnott
Larry Ballenger
Walter Becker
Dick Berry
Ron Berry
Wayne Coombs
Sally Cummins
Ted Cummins
Nan Hatch
Jim Hewett
David Hudson
Clifford Larson
Carroll Parten
Marilyn Patterson
Rita-Lou Reid
Russ Reid

Lyla White
Mel White

Without my husband, children, friends and acquaintances, *Happily Ever After* would, indeed, be very difficult and writing this book would have been impossible.

Introductory Remarks

The philosophies that I espouse and the procedures that I recommend in this book are a result of my own experience as a parent, teacher, school administrator and children's minister. Each concept is based on first-hand experience and encounters with children of all races, religions, and socioeconomic backgrounds ranging in age from birth to twelve years of age. Although the concepts can be applied to people of other ages, they are mostly applicable to children twelve and under.

All of the stories and anecdotal material in this book are true. However, in some cases, the names and places have been changed "to protect the innocent" which, in most cases, are the children.

The procedures that I recommend in this book obviously will not work for everyone. Every parent must be true to himself or herself doing only those things that he or she feels comfortable doing. What is right for one parent may not always be right for another. Thus, words like "should," "do," and "don't" are meant to be regarded as suggestions only and not absolutes.

For those who are offended because the English language uses the generic "man" when it means person, let me say that because there are no acceptable alternatives at this point, I consistently use the words "he," "him," and "his" throughout the book to indicate either or both genders. This is done in accordance with our present language structure and in no way is it to be construed to represent a belief that men are superior to women.

1

In the Beginning . . .

Defining Self-Concept

I was twenty-five years old and had been married five years before my first baby was born. I had waited a long time and I wanted everything to be perfect. One month and ten days after conception, I rushed to the doctor's office for the pregnancy test. It was positive. The next day I began making plans for the baby's arrival. Lime green and lemon yellow were the "in" colors for that year, so I decided to use them for the baby's room. Everything was perfectly color-coordinated—right down to the last diaper pin.

I brought the little pink baby home, dressed in his lime-green kimono, and wrapped in his lemon-yellow blanket. Everything was so perfect! Every person who came to see the baby could not help but notice and comment on the fact that everything was so beautifully coordinated. It was obvious to everyone that I was a marvelous mother. (After all, would a terrible mother spend as much time as I did making sure that everything matched?)

We lived very happily in our lime-green and lemon-yellow world, but as Christopher got older, the colors went "out" and I had to shift into another gear. The transition was relatively smooth. Before Chris knew what was happening, he was completely re-color-coded into red, white, and blue. Once in a while he would put up a fuss saying that he didn't like his clothes, but his complaints were soon squelched when I assured him that it was for *his* sake that I dressed him the way I did. "After all," I told him, "I want you to be proud of yourself and I want others to like you and respond well to you, and that's why you must be neat and clean." Besides, I thought to myself subconsciously, when you look good, I look good too!

Time passed. One day we were hurriedly getting Chris dressed for preschool. We were struggling to pull a blue turtleneck sweater over his head— (it matched his red, white, and blue plaid pants) . "I hate this sweater!" Chris protested. "Why are you making me wear it?" "It's for *your* sake, Chris," I shouted back. Chris paused for a moment, looked me straight in the eyes, and quietly responded, "No, mommy, it's not for *my* sake, it's for *your* sake!"

I had been caught with my hand in the cookie jar! Only I wasn't stealing cookies, I was stealing my son's right to be his own person. I wanted other people to think I was a good mother and I was "using" my son to prove it!

Today, when Christopher walks out of the house, I hold my breath and bite my tongue. The "in" thing is to wear old beat-up clothes: the more holes, the more valuable. I cringe and my friends raise their eyebrows, but Chris's friends think that he dresses "neat" and what's more important, Chris feels good about himself.

I may not have admitted it several years ago, but that's what's really important—a child who feels good and thinks well of himself, a child with a positive self-concept.

Perhaps the most crucial responsibility of any parent is to help his child develop a positive self-concept.

There are four things that influence a child's self-concept. They are:

- Who the child thinks he is;
- Who other people think he is;
- Who the child wishes he could be;
- Who the child really is.

Life is less complicated and more productive when who *you* think you are, who *others* think you are, who you *wish* you were, and who you *really* are, are all the same. A person experiences a great deal of conflict, frustration, and anxiety when all of these things are different.

I know this is true because of my own life. Many people think that I am an extrovert. I wish I were one because the people that I would like to please enjoy me as an extrovert. However, being an extrovert is extremely difficult for me, so I think of myself as being an introvert. In reality, I guess I'm a combination of the two. But the conflict and difficulty come in when I try to "be myself" and yet live up to the expectations of other people.

For me to think of and accept myself as an introvert, for others to think of and accept me as an introvert, for me to want to be an introvert, and for me to really be an introvert would be ideal.

Achieving the ideal is not an impossibility. I've known children who have had nearly "ideal" situations. . . . I once had a boy in my class that was very well liked and received by the other children. The story that I tell about Jerry involves only one facet of his personality, but it's representative of his total being. Jerry was a kid who "had it all together." One week before school began, I met Jerry's mother at a PTA luncheon. "You're going to love having Jerry in your class," she told me. "He's delightfully creative!"

On the first day of school the children were asked to write down their name, age, and greatest asset. (Naturally, I had to explain what *asset* meant.) A few minutes passed, then Jerry raised his hand. "How do you spell *creativity?*" he asked.

In the months that followed, I was delighted to find that Jerry was all that he and his mother claimed he was. Halfway through the year, the class was asked to write a story entitled, "I wish I were . . ." Jerry wrote, "I wish I were a person who could think up great ideas, because it is the funnest thing I do!" Jerry, along with everyone else, thought that he was creative. He produced accordingly and enjoyed doing so. Jerry's situation was what I call *ideal*. Obviously, bringing this ideal into existence is the goal, but where do you begin?

I believe that you begin with the self-concept, or "Who a person thinks he is." In reality, a person usually becomes what he thinks he is. "As a man thinketh in his heart, so is he!" If a person feels good about what he has become, others will accept him.

Summary

A. Self-esteem is what a child thinks of himself.
B. There are four things which influence a child's self-concept:
  1. Who the child thinks he is.
  2. Who other people think he is.
  3. Who the child wishes he could be.
  4. Who the child really is.
C. Life is less complicated and more productive when all four of these things are the same. This is an ideal situation.
D. Achieving the ideal is not an impossibility. To help a child achieve the ideal, one should begin by helping the child develop a positive self-concept—who he thinks he is.

2

No Trespassing on Me!

Developing Self-Concept

The first step in helping a child develop a positive self-concept is to BELIEVE IN YOURSELF.

I have a friend who came from a family of five children. The home that the family lived in was always a mess. My friend was so embarrassed because of the condition of the house and, as a child, would often make excuses to her friends about how things looked. When she grew up she became obsessed with perfection. She imposed this perfection on her children, insisting that they *never* get dirty. To complicate matters, she did not allow them to play in the house for fear that it would get dirty. My friend told me that her efforts were for the sake of her children. "I don't want them to feel inferior like I did!" she told me. Little did she realize that her perfectionism was a compensation for *her* feelings of inferiority, not the feelings of inferiority of her children.

Stories like this one are typical. So often we as parents force things upon our children, saying that it is for their good when, in fact, it is really for our own. Thus our unfilled needs or feelings of inadequacy are imposed upon our children—often without realizing it.

This is why I consider *believing in yourself* to be the very first step in developing a child's self-concept. Before a child's self-concept can be developed into a positive one, it is essential that the parents have a positive concept of themselves. Many times parents are disappointed with who they are and what they are doing with their lives. They find themselves so busy trying to live up to everyone else's expectations that they have not had the privilege of living their own lives.

Unfortunately, when they have a child they subconsciously view the situation as an opportunity to live the life that they were never allowed to live. They view their child's life as a second chance for themselves. Statements like, "My child is going to have everything I didn't have," or "My child is going to be everything I wasn't," are the way this is often expressed.

Have you ever watched men at Little League baseball games? Or a mother at a ballet or piano recital? It is so important to them that their child succeed. In many cases the child may not care, but to the parents, the child's success or failure becomes their own success or failure.

Recently I found myself in a tough situation. An eighteen-year-old boy had come to me seeking encouragement to become a teacher of four- and five-year-old children. I had watched Steve work with young children before and was tremendously impressed with his abilities. "Steve," I told him, "you would make a fantastic teacher!" "Yeah, but how many *real men* work with little kids?" he replied. I went on to explain how important I felt it was to have men working with young children, how more men were going into the children's field and that it was considered by many to be an honorable thing to do.

Before I knew what hit me, Steve had talked me into giving the same pitch to his dad, who was apparently trying to discourage him from becoming a teacher.

Steve arranged for his father and I to get together. The session had a tense beginning. "No son of mine is going to do a woman's job!" the father began. Halfway through my defensive response to his statement, I stopped. "Mr. Del," I asked, "if you could live your life over and if you could do anything or be anything you wanted, what would that be?" Caught off guard, he thought for a moment and then replied, "A professional ball player. And I could have made it, too! I was good enough, but I never received encouragement from anyone. Everyone else had plans for my life! That's what makes me so sick about Steve," he continued. "He could be a professional ball player. Heaven only knows I've given him every break a kid could ever want. He could make it. He's big enough and good enough, but he won't even try. There's nothing I'd like more than to see him have the chance to do what I always wanted to do."

Unfortunately, many parents find themselves in Mr. Del's place. To believe in yourself, after living a life that has revolved around the expectations of others, is a difficult thing to do. But nonetheless, it is a must and it is possible. It begins with each of us concentrating on who we are, not on who we wish we were or who other people wish we were, but who we actually are.

I am a unique individual, created by God for a special purpose. When God made me he threw away the mold. Think of it! There has never been, nor will there ever be another human being just like me. I am the first and last of a kind. Nothing explains my uniqueness better than this poem.*

Egomania

I saw it in a book, In a zoology book—
"Every individual is absolutely unique,
The first and last of its identical kind."
Unique! The first and last!
Never anybody else just like me!

---

* From *Will the Real Teacher Please Stand Up* by Mary Greer and Bonnie Rubinstein, p. 22. Copyright © 1972 by Goodyear Publishing Company. Used by permission.

Never! Never!
I am the only one just like me,
I am a race by myself.
When I die the world will have lost me—Forever.
Spermatogonia, spermatocytes, spermatozoa.
Oogonia, oocytes, ova—
Then oosperm!
And the three hundred thousand billionth chance
Produced me!
Think of it! The three hundred thousand billionth possi-
   bility—
Think if it hadn't happened.
But it did—and never can again. Never.
Chromosomes, chromomeres, chromogen, enzymes,
Protoplasm, germ plasm, cytoplasm, somato-plasm,
Permutation, maturation, segregation, differentiation,
Synapsis, mitosis, ontogeny, phylogeny—
All the combinations and changes and chances
That made me
Can never again come together
Exactly the same.
I am a person of distinction.
I am I.
I am that I am.

Not only am I unique, I am valuable.

I read an article some time ago in a newspaper entitled, "Teenage Suicides Traced to the American Fairytale." The article told about Amy, a fifteen-year-old girl who had always received straight A's in school. Her parents were extremely upset when she came home with a "B" in one of her subjects. "If I fail in what I do," Amy told her parents, "I fail in what I am." The message was part of her suicide note. Amy had ceased to feel valuable. The article went on to cite the words of Dr. Treffert, the director of the Winnebago Mental Health Institute at Oshkosh, Wisconsin. He placed part of the blame for the sharp increase in teenage suicides on what he called the "American Fairytale."

The Fairytale, as he described it, had several themes, but the two important ones were (1) more possessions mean more happiness, and (2) a person who does or produces more is more important.

The article went on to admonish parents to stop valuing themselves and their children on the basis of what they own and/or what they have done.

To do this is to recognize our value as persons. I may not feel valuable because, according to the world's standards, I may not be. I may not have a Ph.D. I may not be a raving beauty. I may not have a gorgeous home with three cars in the garage. This does not mean that I am not valuable. God does not measure a person's worth by the world's standards.

You and I are valuable by virtue of the fact that we were created by God. Everything that God creates has value, meaning, and purpose. You were put on the earth for a special purpose that only you can fulfill. You are important to the world that you live in, no matter how large or small it is.

Besides being unique and valuable, you share an equality with all other human beings. This is difficult to comprehend because some people are born millionaires while others are born into poverty. How then is equality achieved? Every person is equal because God creates him with the potential and ability to achieve all that he wants him to achieve and, for you, that is to:

- Love Him.
- Love yourself.
- Love others.

Every person created by God has the potential to achieve these three goals, no matter who they are or what situation they may be born into.

The second step in helping a child develop a positive self-concept is BELIEVE IN YOUR CHILD.

Believing in your child means that you believe in him for the same reasons that you believe in yourself. Your child is also a unique individual, created by God for a special purpose. He is unique, he is valuable, and he is equal to all other human beings.

The third step in helping your child develop a positive self-concept is GET YOUR CHILD TO BELIEVE IN YOU (to respect you).

Compliments and criticism always carry more weight when they come from people we respect. This is true for children, too. If your child respects you, he is more likely to be affected by your affirmations of him and your desires for him to, in some cases, change his behavior. Gaining your child's respect is not an optional part of the program. If you are to have any influence on his life in a positive way, he must respect you.

I was shopping in a supermarket one day when I overheard a young mother in the next aisle yelling at her child. "I'll teach you to respect me!" she shouted as she proceeded to spank the child. "That's what you think!" I said to myself. "You may be able to teach your child how to *show* respect, but it is impossible for you to teach your child *to* respect you." This is because respect, like love, is something that comes from within. A child can be forced to show love and respect, but how he really feels is up to him! One should not confuse *fear* with *respect*. Some parents think that they have taught their child to respect them when in reality they have taught their child to fear them. When a child respects a parent, he responds positively to the parent because he has feelings of honor and esteem for the parent. On the other hand, when a child fears a parent, he functions out of dread and anxiety over what might happen to him if his parent does not approve of his actions.

Many parents think that they are automatically due respect from their children simply because they are the parents. This is not necessarily true. Respect is something one earns. No one automatically inherits it because of his or her age, status, or position in life.

I made this statement to a group of parents some time ago, and before I was able to put the period at the end of the sentence, a parent challenged me. "God has put parents in authority over their children and this automatically demands that children respect their parents," he told me. Sadly, I related to him several of the terrible family situations that I had been exposed to: situations where children had been beaten beyond the point of recognition, or where children were encouraged (and in some cases, forced) to steal, lie, and cheat. Did the parents of these children deserve their child's respect simply because they were the parents?

Respect is something that each individual must earn for himself. How does one earn respect from others?

Recently I approached a group of children in search of the answer to the question, "What makes you respect the adults that you respect?" In the thirty-minute session that followed, this is what they said (taken verbatim from the tape-recording made of the session) :

> JOHN: Well, sometimes I think grownups are kind of fake, and that makes it hard to respect them. Do you know what I mean?
>
> JOY: Not exactly. What do you mean by "fake"?
>
> JOHN: (Pause) Well, like my mother always laughs at my grandpa's jokes when she's with him, but then when grandpa is gone, she tells my dad that she thinks that grandpa's jokes are dumb.
>
> SARAH: Or like my mother. . . . Meg—that's our neighbor—got her hair cut. My mom said that it looked cute. Then mother told Barbara—that's our other neighbor—that Meg shouldn't have gotten her hair cut because it looked terrible.

Larry: I think it's fake when they [grownups] act different around other grownups.

Joy: What do you mean?

Larry: Like my mom and dad and my friends' moms and dads. They act one way around kids and then different around adults.

Joy: Do you feel that to respect someone, they should not be fake—they should be real?

The group: Yes!

Joy: What is another thing that makes you want to respect the adults that you respect?

Mandy: I respect someone who tells the truth.

John: No one is perfect. No one always always always tells the truth.

Mandy: The thing that's not fair is everyone knows when kids don't tell the truth, but when adults don't tell the truth, no one knows!

The group: Yeah!

Bart: My mom lies to my dad sometimes, but it all evens out because my dad lies to my mom. It's kinda funny.

Cindy: I know my mom and dad would never admit it, but they lie. At least I think they do. Like when my mom tells me to answer the phone and tell the people that she's not home when she really is. That's a lie, isn't it?

Sarah: Yeah! My mom lies. She tells her friends that she promises never to tell anyone the secrets they tell her, but she never keeps her promise. She tells everyone the secrets.

Joy: Do you think it is important for adults to be honest if they are to be respected?

The group: Yes!

JOY: Is there anything else an adult should do or be in order to gain your respect?

BART: It's hard to respect someone when one minute they act one way and the next minute they act another way.

JOY: What do you mean?

BART: Sometimes my dad lets me do some things and other times he won't. Like sometimes he won't let me play with Joey because he says Joey is a bad influence. Then other times if I beg real hard, he says OK.

JOHN: My parents always change their mind, too. It all depends. . . .

THE GROUP: Yeah!

JOY: Depends on what?

BART: What kind of mood they're in.

CINDY: Or how tired they are! When my mom is tired, she's grouchy!

CAROLYN: Or what time of day it is. My dad is grouchy right after he comes home from work.

JOY: So you think that adults should be consistent if they want to be respected?

LARRY: What does "consistent" mean?

JOY: It means saying what you mean, then sticking to what you have said. It also means that a person acts pretty much the same all the time. You know what to expect from a person that is consistent.

JOHN: Mr. Jacobson [their school principal] is consistent!

MARK: Yeah! We know what to expect from him!

JOY: Do you respect him?

THE GROUP: Yeah!

BART: Yes, adults that I respect are consistent.

THE GROUP: Yeah!

In subsequent sessions involving other groups of children, the same three expectations were revealed. Children expected the adults that they respected to be real, honest, and consistent. Another expectation that had not been uncovered in the original session was fairness. Children also respect adults that are fair. One girl expressed it this way: "Some adults are so unfair, and when they are unfair it just shows that they're too dumb to think straight!"

When you really think about it, a child does not demand any more than anyone else does. Adults wanting to gain the respect of their peers are required to be real, honest, consistent, and fair. Why should it be any different for the adult who wants to gain the respect of a child?

The fourth step in helping a child develop a positive self-concept is GET YOUR CHILD TO BELIEVE IN HIMSELF.

After believing in yourself, believing in your child, and getting your child to believe in you, then you have to get him to believe in himself. Begin by teaching him who he is.

Your child is like other human beings—especially you. Cindy Herbert wrote a book entitled, *I See a Child*. These two poems were taken from her book and are typical of a child's feelings.*

Tell Me a Story

Tell me about when you were my age.
Tell me about your family and your friends.
Tell me what you did all day when you were a kid.
Tell me again about that time you got into trouble
And didn't know why.
I'm so relieved to know you used to be a kid, too.

Sameness

Supposing we had something in common.
Supposing we liked the same thing—

---

* From *I See a Child* by Cindy Herbert, copyright © 1973 by Learning About Growing. Used by permission of Doubleday and Co., Inc.

A sunny day, A sport,
Wind blowing through the trees.
Supposing we laughed together.
Do you suppose we might?

Children need to know that they are human and, because
they are, they are like other human beings both physically
and emotionally. There is no reason for them to ever be embarrassed or ashamed of their normal bodily functions—vom-
iting, going to the toilet, etc. There is also no reason for them
to be embarrassed or ashamed of their feelings. Everyone
cries, everyone gets angry, everyone has the same kinds of
emotions.

Children can also be taught another concept: They, like
other human beings, possess a combination of assets and
faults. NO ONE IS PERFECT. The fourth thing that makes a
child like other people is the fact that he has the ability to do
well, but yet he sometimes makes mistakes.

One day I had an opportunity to visit a private school that
had the reputation of being "the toughest school to get into
and out of in Southern California." Admittance to the school
required high scores on five different tests. To graduate, one
had to pass a series of seven difficult tests.

Needless to say, the students in this school were expected
to produce. Mistakes, no matter how large or how small,
were frowned upon.

I visited the first-grade classroom during a ten-minute
period of "free play." While I was there, I watched a small
group of children listening to a record. Attached to the
record player were six sets of headphones. The children
wearing the headphones were the only ones that could hear
the record. I was intrigued as I watched them. They obviously liked the particular song they were listening to, because they played it over and over again. In fact, they didn't
play any other song during the entire period of free play.
As they listened to the song, they giggled and their eyes
sparkled.

"What song could be so appealing?" I asked myself.

When the period was over, the children returned to their seats, leaving the record on the record player. I had made a mental note of the fact that the song they were playing was on the third band of the record, so I went over to the record player and picked up the record. It was a Sesame Street recording and the song they had been playing was "Everyone Makes Mistakes." The song says in a clever way that "Big people, small people . . . matter of fact all people" make mistakes.

As well as possessing assets, children have faults. In addition to having the potential to do well, children have the potential to make mistakes. These things are nothing a child should be embarrassed about or ashamed of. Helping your child develop his self-concept includes helping him accept and appreciate his humanness.

When you teach your child who he is, you will want to teach him that, as a human being, he is like other human beings in many ways, but as an individual, he is also delightfully different. The situation that he was born into, the gifts and abilities that God has given him, and the purpose for which he was born are unlike those of any other person in the world.

A child that is encouraged to accept his humanness and yet appreciate his individuality is well on his way to developing a positive self-concept.

In addition to teaching a child who he is, it is important to *show your child that you value him*. Your child will know that you value him when you begin to value the things that he values. (This is a tough one for me!) Lisa's collection of Sowbugs—which she keeps in a quart jar on top of her dresser—and Christopher's collection of rocks—that he calls "precious stones," imported by him all the way to our house from the neighbor's graveled driveway—are about to drive me crazy! But to sneak them into the trash would only confirm their suspicions that I could not possibly value their precious treasures. I expect them to value my hand-knitted sofa pillows; why shouldn't I value their priceless possessions? Valuing a person's things is part of valuing him.

It is also important to value a child's opinion and perception of things. When you're moping around the house because you found out that your raise didn't come through, you really don't feel much like listening to anyone—especially a five-year-old girl who's loaded with advice like, "Why don't you tell that man [your boss] that he's not being fair? And why don't you ask him how he would feel if *he* didn't get a raise?"

Sometimes it's hard to appreciate a child's opinion and perception of things, but even if the advice doesn't make sense to us, we still need to value the process that the child's mind went through to come up with the advice. We need to respond to our child with statements like, "I appreciate your being able to think and come up with an opinion," or "I think I can see how you would think that way."

In addition to valuing the things a child values, and valuing his opinion and perceptions, we must value his creations and accomplishments. Many a parent has crushed his child without meaning to by tossing the child's "creation" into the wastepaper basket along with the trash. Another crusher is the familiar "What's that?" question parents ask when their child presents them with one of his special paintings.

But even worse than these are some things I catch myself doing when I'm not thinking. Things like remaking my son's bed after he has spent 15 minutes making it, or recleaning the tub after my daughter, filled with good intentions, just used half a can of Ajax to clean it for me. My kids always stop me in the middle of the act with, "What's the matter with the way *I* did it?" When a child's creations and accomplishments are continually rejected, the child loses the motivation to continue creating and accomplishing.

One of the most important things that must be valued is a child's feelings: his agonies, his ecstacies, his joys, and his defeats. It's not fair to put him down with statements like: "It's silly to feel that way!" "It's not that big of a deal!" or "Don't be childish." If he considers the situation to be a "big deal," it should be a "big deal" to us, too!

Here's another poem from *I See a Child* that illustrates what I mean.*

Ask a Stupid Question

You don't make fun of me
like some grown-ups do.
I know some of the things I
worry about are silly;
That my fears don't make sense.
But those things are real to me.
I'm glad you don't tell me they're dumb.

There is a third thing one should do in order to get a child to believe in himself. *Do not allow him to be a failure.* I did *not* say that you must never allow him to fail. There is a difference. A person can fail without becoming a failure. I once saw a clever bumper sticker on a car which read, "Being a failure is not falling down, it is remaining there when you have fallen!"

A lot of successful people have failed before they finally succeeded.

- Thomas Edison failed approximately 5,000 times before he came up with the world's first practical light bulb.
- King Gillette invented the safety razor in one hour . . . and spent the next seven years developing a market for it.
- F. W. Woolworth's first three stores went bankrupt.
- And then there was Abraham Lincoln . . .
  1831   Failed in business
  1832   Defeated for the legislature

---

* From *I See a Child* by Cindy Herbert, copyright © 1973 by Learning About Growing. Used by permission of Doubleday and Co., Inc.

1833 Again failed in business
1834 Elected to the legislature
1835 His sweetheart died
1836 Had a nervous breakdown
1840 Defeated for elector
1843 Defeated for congress
1846 Elected to congress
1848 Defeated for congress
1855 Defeated for senate
1856 Defeated for vice-president
1858 Defeated for senate
1860 ELECTED PRESIDENT

These men failed, but they were successful people. It's possible to help a child be a successful person even though he has failed—if you make his failure an educational experience. Every failure has a hidden lesson. If you help your child learn that lesson you will make his failure a positive experience instead of a negative one. Also, do not allow guilt feelings to persist in your child over a failure. Encourage him with the fact that everyone fails sometimes . . . it really helps when you share with him about some of your failures.

The last thing I would recommend in helping a child develop his self-concept is to *see that he experiences success.* This can be done by helping him establish goals that he can achieve. I have known children to be so unrealistic in setting their goals that failure could not possibly be avoided. But children are not the only source for unrealistic goals. I've also known parents, relatives, and teachers, to establish some pretty unrealistic goals for children and then heap guilt upon them when they failed to meet up to their expectations. If failure is to be avoided, goals, no matter who establishes them, must be realistic.

Also, success is a pretty sure thing when a child is effectively using his natural gifts and abilities. Help him discover his gifts and then encourage him to use them.

Summary

There are four steps to follow in order to develop a child's self-concept.

A. Believe in yourself because you are:
1. unique,
2. valuable,
3. equal.

B. Believe in your child because he is:
1. unique,
2. valuable,
3. equal.

C. Get your child to believe in you (respect you) by being:
1. real,
2. honest,
3. consistent,
4. fair.

D. Get your child to believe in himself by:
1. Teaching him who he is.
   a. He is like other human beings physically and emotionally. Like other human beings, he possesses a combination of assets and faults, and, like other human beings, he has the ability to do well, but he also makes mistakes.
   b. He is an individual because of the situation he was born into, his gifts and abilities, and the purpose for which he was born.
   c. He is a special child of God.
2. Valuing him and his values, opinions, perceptions, creations, accomplishments, and feelings.
3. Not allowing him to be a failure.
   a. Help your child make his failures into positive learning experiences.
   b. Don't allow him to have persistent guilt feelings over his failures.

4. Seeing that he experiences success.
   a. That he sets goals that he can accomplish. (Make sure that parents, relatives, and teachers do the same.)
   b. That he is effectively using his gifts and abilities.

3

Getting Down to the Nitty-Gritty

Meeting a Child's Basic Needs

It was 9:30 A.M. on the first day of public school. Class had not yet begun. I was standing at the door welcoming each child into the classroom when a loud commotion erupted just outside. Two boys were screaming obscenities to one another. Before I knew what was happening, the larger of the two boys had the smaller one pinned to the ground and was beating him to a pulp. I rushed over and, using every ounce of strength I had, pulled the boys apart. The big boy turned on me and began kicking me in the shin. "Get your hands off of me!" he shrieked. "I hate teachers and I hate you!"

Believe it or not, this is the beginning of a beautiful story. . . .

Later in the morning I learned that the boy responsible for my bruised shin was none other than "Terrible Tim," a name given to Tim by his peers. Although Tim was in my third grade class, he should have been in the fifth. He had been held back two years. The fact that Tim was two years older and bigger than the other children made it possible for him to terrorize them. They couldn't stand him—and neither could I.

After several futile attempts at getting Tim transferred to another classroom—I was a beginning teacher and I argued

that a "more experienced teacher could handle Tim better"
—I gave up and resigned myself to the fact that I was going
to have to face up to the problem. But where was I to begin?

It was obvious that before I could plan my strategy I had
to find out what I was up against, so I made arrangements to
visit Tim at his home.

It was 4:00 in the afternoon when I knocked on the door
of a small run-down house in the "bad" section of town. No
one came to the door, so I walked around to the back of the
house where I found Tim trying to hide from me. The first
few moments of our encounter seemed like forever. Our conversation was strained, but then a miracle happened. Tim
began to talk. "Mom's inside," he told me. "She's sleeping
'cause she's gotta work tonight."

That was all it took. For one hour Tim poured out his
soul. He told me about his father leaving and his mother
going to work as a waitress in what I later learned was a top-
less bar. He told me about her working all night. He told
me about the two younger sisters that he was responsible for.
It was his job to feed them dinner (TV dinners) and breakfast (cold cereal and milk). It was also his job to get them in
bed at night and up in the morning for school. Many nights
he would be left all night at home alone with his two younger
sisters.

Before I left Tim, I made him promise to see me after
school the next day. When the dismissal bell rang that next
day, Tim was up at my desk before the other children had
cleared out of the room.

When we were finally alone, I sat him down on a chair in
front of me. "Tim," I said, "I care for you and I want to
help you!" In the forty-five minutes that followed, I pre-
sented Tim a contract that I had prepared the night before.
The contract was based on Tim's needs. To begin with, he
had physical needs that were not being met. His diet was
terrible and his body needed rest. In addition, no one was
meeting his emotional needs. Everyone ran the other way
when they saw him coming. He felt unloved, he was not

respected or trusted, and his home-life was insecure. Furthermore, failure had hindered him from having his intellectual and creative needs met. Tim's life was a bottomless pit of unfulfilled needs.

The contract was simple. It included the following: Every day I was to provide Tim with a nutritious "sack" breakfast. Arrangements were to be made for him to eat the breakfast in the nurse's office where, after he was finished eating, he was allowed to relax or sleep until he felt he was rested enough to return to the classroom. This was designed to meet a few of Tim's physical needs and is the first step in getting a "deprived child" squared away. In regard to schoolwork, Tim would be paid one nickel for every completed assignment and he could earn additional money by staying after school and helping me with miscellaneous jobs. (During the conversation I had with him at his home, I learned that money was important to him.)

Tim signed the contract and the program began the next day. While he was in the nurse's office on the first day, I talked with the other kids in the class. "How many of you have ever been beaten up or bullied by Tim?" I asked. Nearly every child raised his hand. "How did you feel about it?" I continued. Responses of hostility and resentment rang out from the group. "If something could be done to stop Tim from bullying you and hitting you, would you be pleased?" "Yes!" they shrieked. I questioned further. "Would you help to make it possible?" It was silent for a moment and then one of the girls spoke up. "How?"

It took me nearly twenty minutes to answer her question. This is basically what I said. . . .

"Who can tell me what we learned about plants yesterday?" Nearly every hand went up. One child was chosen to answer. "We learned that plants need soil, water, air, and light." Another child continued, "Yeah, and if the plant doesn't get those things, it can't grow." "It'll die," a third child added.

"Good!" I said. "Knowing what you know about plants is

going to help you understand Tim." In spite of the puzzled looks on their faces, I went on. "People are like plants. They need certain things in order to stay alive and grow. Just like the plant, they need food, water, and air, but that's not all they need. They need things like love, respect, trust. . . ." Trying not to lose the class, I stopped and then addressed a question to one of the girls. "Jennifer, tell us again what happened in the experiment you did when you put your bean plant in the dark closet." "It grew real tall trying to find light. Then, when it couldn't find any, it became weak and died," she answered. "But what has that got to do with Tim?" one of the boys asked.

"Tim is like Jennifer's bean plant," I said. "He's not getting what he needs and so he's going after it. He may not be going after it in the best possible way, but it's all he knows how to do. Among many other things, Tim needs to be noticed. When you do not pay attention to him, he trys to get you to notice him by hitting or bullying you. You fight back, Tim feels unwanted, and the whole thing keeps going on and on. It looks something like this" (I drew the following diagram on the blackboard) :

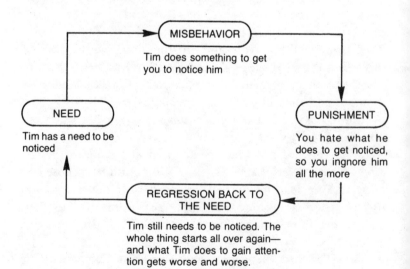

I continued. "If you don't want Tim to bully you, you've got to help him break the vicious cycle by doing something like this" (I drew a second diagram on the board) :

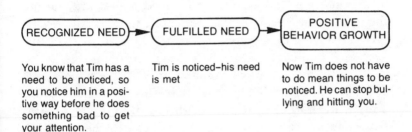

RECOGNIZED NEED	FULFILLED NEED	POSITIVE BEHAVIOR GROWTH
You know that Tim has a need to be noticed, so you notice him in a positive way before he does something bad to get your attention.	Tim is noticed–his need is met	Now Tim does not have to do mean things to be noticed. He can stop bullying and hitting you.

Maybe every child in the class did not understand all of the ramifications of my diagrams, but they did understand enough to ask me what kind of needs Tim had.

"We all have the same basic needs," I told them. "In addition to our physical needs—food, water, air, rest—we have emotional needs. We need to be loved, respected, and trusted. We also need to feel secure. Besides our physical and emotional needs, we have intellectual and creative needs. We need to think and create!"

I went on: "We can't possibly meet all of Tim's needs, but we sure can meet some of them by loving, accepting, and being kind to him."

After a brief explanation of Tim's contract and how the class could help make it effective, the children agreed to help me. "It's worth it!" one boy said. "I'm sick of having bruises on my back!"

In the months that followed, Tim became a new person while he was at school. He ended up making A's and B's and being well liked by almost everyone in the class.

But the "perfect ending" didn't happen until several months ago when I was doing a childrens' show in a shopping mall. When the show was over, two six-foot boys walked up to me. I recognized one immediately, but the other I wasn't sure about. "Mrs. Cox?" they began (that was my name at the time I was teaching). "Yes." I responded. "Do you remember us?" they continued. "We were in your class about nine years ago!" "Why, yes!" I beamed. "How are you doing?" Bob, the one I recognized, spoke up: "Well, we just graduated from high school. I was All-C.I.F. in football this year, and Tim here, well, he graduated with honors."

So much can be learned from the story of "Terrible Tim." Every form of punishment imaginable had been inflicted on Tim in an effort to correct his misbehavior, but it wasn't until certain needs were met that Tim's behavior began to improve. It is true that not all misbehavior is the result of unfulfilled needs, but much of it is. Many times the trauma of having to correct a child's misbehavior can be avoided by meeting the child's needs *before* the misbehavior occurs. In Tim's case, it was giving him much-needed love and attention before he went after it in a socially unacceptable way.

But avoiding or correcting misbehavior is not the only reason for seeing that a child's needs are met. Certain things are required by a person in order to survive and grow. Without these things, survival and growth are almost impossible. Because every person tends toward survival and growth of some kind, every person has needs. When these needs are met the person survives and growth occurs. Meeting your child's needs makes it possible for him to survive and grow.

The first step in meeting a child's needs is to become aware of what his needs are and how they can be met. Although all of us share the same basic needs, *how* these needs are met varies with every person.

A good illustration of this concept can be found in the gift that my brother gave me last year for Christmas. Ron had taken a pottery class and had "hand thrown" a pot for me. To complete the gift, he had planted a beautiful plant in the pot. I had not had much success with raising plants before, but this time I was highly motivated. Thanks to my experience as a third grade teacher, I knew that all plants needed water, air, soil, and light. So I generously watered the plant and set it out on the back porch to soak up the sun. Within three days, all of the leaves on the plant were brown. Frantically I rushed the plant to the local nursery. "What went wrong?" I asked. "I gave it everything it needed!" Carefully, he examined the plant. "I'm sure you did," he responded, "but you gave it too much sun. The plant was an indoor plant." "Was?" I asked quizzically. The nursery-man sadly shook his head. "Was. It's a goner now!"

Knowing what the plant needed was not enough. I needed to know the specifics of how these needs were to have been met. For you to know that your child needs security is not enough. You need to know specifically what will meet this need. For example, like all children, both Christopher and Lisa have a need to feel secure. For Christopher, routine— following the same schedule every day—makes him feel secure. Lisa hates routine! According to her, doing the same thing every day is boring. Her sense of security comes from being in control. When she is a part of deciding what is going to happen to her, she feels secure.

Knowing how to meet a child's needs comes from knowing the child. No one can better tell you how to meet your child's needs than your child himself. He may not be able to verbalize this, but you will be able to discover what his needs are and how to meet them by observing which situations he prefers, which situations he responds best in, and which situations provide the maximum amount of growth with the least amount of trauma. Observing his misbehavior and trying to determine *why* it is happening is another good method of discovering the child's needs and how to meet them. In addition to observing, listening is also crucial. Listening to a child's preferences, his requests, and demands is a good way to discern his inner needs.

"Oh, I listen to them all right!" a mother once told me

sarcastically. "But if I would give in to all of his preferences, requests, and demands, he'd be so spoiled rotten that you couldn't stand to be around him!" Unfortunately, too many parents would wholeheartedly agree. Somehow, they've gotten the impression that "giving in" to a child in any way is the beginning of a downhill run leading to total permissiveness.

I do not advocate that a parent give into his child's every desire, but I do advocate that preferences, requests, and demands that are realistic, reasonable, and necessary for the growth and development of the child should—indeed, must —be met.

Ignoring a child's preferences and meeting his needs in the way *we* feel they should be met does not always produce positive results. I once knew a young boy who was musically inclined and physically coordinated. He preferred to meet his need for physical activity by dancing. "Horrors!" his parents thought. "We can tolerate him becoming anything but a dancer!" For several years they provided him with every kind of lesson imaginable. He became quite adept at swimming, gymnastics, skating, and tennis, but his need to dance was never met. Finally his frustration over not being able to dance began to drastically affect his behavior. His parents were forced into seeking help for him. Family counseling and therapy resulted in the boy being able to dance. Within weeks his behavior problem disappeared.

We must not assume that our child's needs can be met in the same way that our own needs are met. Every person's needs must be met in a way that is acceptable to him.

Summary

A. Every child tends toward survival and growth.
B. Every child needs certain things in order to survive and grow.
C. By meeting a child's needs, a parent:

1. Makes it possible for him to survive and grow.
2. Avoids the child misbehaving in an effort to get his needs met.
D. In order to meet a child's needs a parent must:
   1. Know what his needs are (most people share the same basic needs) .
   2. Know how those needs can be met (this will vary with each child) .
E. You can find out how your child's needs can be met by:
   1. Observing which situations
      a. he prefers,
      b. he responds best in,
      c. provide the maximum amount of growth with the least amount of trauma.
   2. Observing his misbehavior and determining *why* he is misbehaving.
   3. Listening to his
      a. preferences,
      b. requests,
      c. demands.
F. Meeting your child's needs is not spoiling him.
G. Do not assume that a child's needs can be met in the same way that an adult's needs are met.

4

Spinach, Bedtime, and Other Yucky Necessities of Life

Meeting a Child's Physical Needs

Last year my son was in kindergarten. Having a child in school was a new experience for me and I know that I was quite anxious about the whole thing. One day Christopher's teacher met me at the door of the classroom when I arrived to pick him up. "Mrs. Wilt," she said, "we need to have a little talk about Christopher." I was stunned. "Certainly!" I said. "Do you have time to talk now?" "No," she replied, "but I can see you in two weeks." "Two weeks!" I thought. "If I have to wait for two weeks to find out what's important enough to warrant a non-scheduled conference, I'll die!" I spoke up: "Can you give me a clue as to what we will be talking about?" "Not now, Mrs. Wilt," she replied. "I'd rather discuss the problem in private when we have more time."

For the next two weeks my imagination ran wild. What "problems" could my precious little angel possibly have? By the time the day of the conference came, I was an emotional wreck. The teacher began the conference by telling me that Chris did not pay attention to much of anything that was go-

47

ing on in the classroom. Furthermore, he was not capable of following directions. The rest of the conference revolved around the data that she had gathered to support her case. Her collection included a stack of Chris's unfinished and/or incorrect work papers. Consistent with the rest of the conference, our meeting ended on a negative note. The teacher concluded by saying, "Chris does not listen well. I tell him one thing and he does something exactly opposite. I think that Christopher needs help. I've done all I can do; I'll have to leave the rest up to you."

By the time I got out to my car, tears were streaming down my face. I cried all the way home. My husband was waiting for me as I arrived. "What shall we do?" I asked him between sobs. "Well, what do you tell other parents to do when their child is misbehaving at school?" he replied. I stopped crying, thought for a moment and then said, "I tell them that no problem is unsolvable, that misbehavior is usually a result of unfulfilled needs." "Well?" he replied.

The next day I made an appointment for Chris to have a physical examination. When a child is misbehaving or has a problem, I always suggest to the parents that they first explore the child's physical needs because a deficiency in this area is relatively easy to diagnose and treat.

From all outward appearances, Chris was healthy and well, but further examination by the doctor revealed that Chris had a hearing loss. The pediatrician referred us to a hearing specialist who, after a series of tests, determined that Chris had a severe hearing loss in both ears. No wonder he wasn't following directions—he couldn't hear them!

I relayed the information to Chris's teacher. She was very cooperative and began speaking louder and more directly to Chris. In addition, she moved him up front during group activities. The doctor placed Chris on medication and began regular treatments to improve his hearing. Within a few months his hearing was back and his behavior problem was gone.

Persecution and punishment would not have been effective in correcting Chris's misbehavior but rather would more likely have complicated things. His problem was a physical one that required medical attention.

Too often children are labeled as unintelligent, uncooperative, immature, and incorrigible when in reality unfulfilled physical needs are preventing them from being and doing all of the positive things that they are capable of doing.

I am not a physician, but I do know that before growth can take place, children must have sufficient amounts of good food, water, air, rest, and exercise. In addition, it is important that, as much as possible, every part of their body functions normally. In cases where normal functioning is not possible, compensations (glasses, hearing aids, environmental modifications, etc.) must be made.

If your child is having problems achieving or if he is misbehaving, your first step in correcting the situation is to determine whether or not all of his physical needs are being met. For an accurate evaluation of this, consult a physician. If the evaluation indicates an unfulfilled need, your second step is to initiate action that will meet this need.

5

Love Conquers a Lot . . .
But Not Quite All!

Meeting a Child's Emotional Needs

Six months ago I qualified for a second Purple Heart for
being wounded in the line of duty. (I received my first medal
for being kicked in the shin by Tim.) This time it was my
left shin and, to make matters worse, I was kicked twice in
the same spot! The offender was Tom, a five-year-old boy
that attended Christopher and Lisa's school.

In celebration of Lisa's birthday I had volunteered to stage
a puppet and magic show for her class and for Christopher's.
On the day of the show, I arrived at the school loaded down
with three boxes. I carried them to the classroom, hoping
that someone would be available to open the door for me.
I'm in luck! I thought to myself as I rounded the corner and
saw a boy standing near the door. "Would you please open
the door for me?" I asked as I approached him. The boy
didn't budge. Thinking that he didn't hear me, I repeated
the question: "Would you please open the door for me?"
Still no response. By this time, the box on the top of the
stack was beginning to slide off. Frantically, I pleaded,

"Could you get that top box for me?" Unphased, the boy watched the box fall, spilling its contents all over the ground. I stood stunned for a moment and then, before I could say anything, the boy kicked me twice in the shin and ran into the classroom. The teacher had heard the crash and hurried to my aid. Seeing the mess on the ground, she shook her head despairingly and said, "Tom strikes again!"

"Tom. . . ." That name sounded familiar to me. I was sure that I had heard it before . . . but where? Then, halfway through the show, I remembered. Tom had been the subject of nearly all of Christopher and Lisa's school stories since the beginning of the school year. "Tom pushed Jonathan off of his bike today" or "Tom knocked Jennifer's tooth out" or "Tom spit on the teacher" they would tell me. It was obvious that Tom had problems.

Later I found out that Tom was living with his aunt until the court could make a decision in the bitter custody feud that had been raging between his parents for over a year. My heart went out to Tom. I committed myself to reaching out to him. Every day when I walked the children to their classrooms, I made a point of giving Tom some desperately needed attention and love. At first, he was suspicious and totally rejected my affection. But, after about three weeks, he began to respond. At the end of two months, he was meeting me at the door with hugs and kisses.

One morning while driving to school, Christopher leaned forward in his seat and said, "Mom, how come is it that everyone hates Tom and he hates everyone? But you love him and he loves you!"

"Chris," I answered, "It's what you call seeing beyond the guilt to the need." "What does that mean?" he asked. "Well, right now Tom does not feel loved," I told him, "and that makes him want to be mean to other people. Instead of hating him for being mean, I feel sorry for him for not feeling loved and I try to be kind to him." Chris slid back into his seat and thought for a moment. Then he leaned forward again. "You know, mom, you could be Jesus' wife!"

That evening, after a "routine Tom story," I asked Christopher a question. "Chris, would you like to help Tom get better?" "How?" he asked. "By being kind to him before he has a chance to be mean. By loving him before he has a chance to hate you." In the conversation that followed, Chris committed himself to a "two-week be-kind-to-Tom program."

Every day on the way to his classroom I reminded Chris of his commitment. Before long, Tom was also greeting Chris at the door with hugs and kisses. Tom and Chris began to like each other very much and at the end of two weeks I was pointing out to Christopher that the program had indeed been a success. "Yeah, mom," he said with a sigh, "I guess love conquers all!"

Unfortunately, I can't take the credit for Chris's statement. I have no idea where he got it, but there's a lot of truth in it. For sure, love is a good way to begin conquering a child's emotional problems.

The Need to Be Loved

A lot has been said about love—and not just recently. I remember asking my dad as a young child, "Why is every song and every movie about love?" His answer: "Because love makes the world go 'round!"

The things that we *love* are the things that we value. It is no different with the people that we love. If we love a person, we value him. This means that he has become worthy of a portion of our time, efforts, and possessions. In sharing these things with him, we communicate to him that he is important to us and that he is loved by us.

For my birthday last year, my husband and children gave me a beautiful ring with their birthstones on it. The ring was too large, and when I went to have it refitted I asked the jeweler, "What makes some stones more expensive than others?" "Their value," she replied. "And what makes one more valuable than another?" I asked. "Their rarity," she said. "The harder a stone is to get, the more valuable it is."

I can't help but think how much this standard applies to one's time, efforts, and possessions. The one thing that we have the least of always seems to be the one thing that our children value and need the most. In my case, it is time. Sharing my possessions and buying the children things is no problem. Working hard to give them a *neat* birthday party or making an effort to do other things for them is also no problem . . . as long as it fits into my schedule! For me, time is very precious because it is so rare.

I was running out of the house one evening, late, as usual, on my way to a meeting. My daughter stopped me at the door. "You're *not* going out again!" she protested. "Yes, sweetie, but if you'll be a good sport about me going, I'll get you a little surprise," I told her. "I don't need a surprise," she said with tears filling her eyes. "I need you home with me!" (This incident gave rise to the only-one-night-out-a-week-for-mommy rule that now exists in our household.)

It would have simplified matters if Lisa could have been "bought off," but she couldn't. Giving up a little of something that was precious to me (sacrificing) was an inevitability. It's all a part of showing a person that you love him. By *sacrificing* I do not mean that you become a martyr and give up *everything* for your child. If you did, you would more than likely develop feelings of hostility and resentment toward your child, and your child would develop feelings of guilt. This isn't going to help anyone!

Whereas time is my most precious commodity, money (possessions) may be someone else's. I know of low-income families where the mother is home all day with the children. The children have all the time they need, but money is hard to come by. In these situations, possessions often become the thing that is valued.

Meeting a child's emotional need for love may mean that

we may have to sacrifice a little. Telling a child that you love him is great, but it's not enough. We have to prove it by our willingness to share with him our time, our efforts, and our possessions.

The Need to Be Respected

Love conquers a lot, but I don't think that it conquers all. A child has other emotional needs—like the need to be respected. By this, I mean he needs to be respected for what he *is*, not for what we want him to be.

Too often, a parent will withhold respect from his child saying, either consciously or unconsciously, "I will respect you after you become the person I want you to become." This is totally contrary to what he expects from anyone else. He would expect another person to be real, honest, consistent, and fair in order to be respected. But when it comes to his own child, it is somehow different. A child who is real, honest, and consistent is usually one who is being himself and this is totally unacceptable to the parent whose expectations and aspirations for his child do not include "being himself."

Mandy is a perfect example of this. (She was one of the girls in the small group that discussed "respect" in chapter two.) Mandy was quite a girl! Intelligent, nice-looking, and, unfortunately for her mother, an aggressive extrovert. To make matters worse, Mandy was athletically inclined. Mandy's mother had aspired to be a model, but had never quite made it. When Mandy was born (she was the last of four children and had three brothers), her mother saw her chance to be a model—through Mandy. She dressed Mandy beautifully and spent a lot of time fixing her hair. According to Mandy, it was a "drag," and she would have preferred short hair anyway, because long hair just got in her way. The worst part for Mandy, though, came when she had to drop her after-school sports so that she could spend more time on her ballet, modeling, and charm classes.

"She'll thank me some day!" her mother told me. "There's nothing more distasteful than a tomboy! I don't see how Mandy could ever expect us to approve of her running around in those dirty old tennis shoes and cut-off jeans. We want something better for her. She's got potential to be a beautiful girl!"

"That's interesting," I said. "I think Mandy *is* a beautiful girl right now. Just the way she is!"

Meeting your child's need for respect means that you respect him right now for what he is, not for what you hope he will become. Let him be himself and respect him for it!

The Need to Trust

Every child also has a need to *trust*. He needs to be able to trust his parents, knowing that what they want for him is really for his good and not for theirs. The vicious "every man for himself" cycle begins all too soon in relationships between parents and children. When a child begins to think that his parents' demands are for their good and not for his own, he begins to get defensive. He also becomes suspicious of everything his parents suggest. It's almost as though he is saying to himself, "If my parents are going to watch out for themselves, I'm going to watch out for *myself*." Parent-child relationships that lack trust are disastrous for both the parents and the child.

It is possible for parents to have a trusting relationship with their child, but it will require some effort on their part. We need to begin with an evaluation of the demands that we are making on our child. Are these demands for our benefit, or are they for his? Most of the time, the demands that we make on our child should be for his good. There are, however, a few occasions when demands for our good are in order. On these occasions, honesty helps. Say to your child, "I am wanting you to do this because *I* need (or want) it." If we are open and honest on these occasions, he will have no need to suspect our demands on other occasions.

A good example of one of those "few occasions" was "bedtime for Lisa" when she was three-and-a half years old. There was a period when Lisa did not require very much sleep. She could go to bed at eleven o'clock, get up at six the next morning and go all day without stopping. She was surviving the schedule just fine. But for my husband and me . . . we were at our wits' end. We never had time to ourselves. Finally, I approached Lisa: "Lisa, you may not be sleepy when Christopher goes to bed, but daddy and I need some time by ourselves. So, when Christopher goes to bed, you'll have to go to bed, too." She fussed about it a little at first and we made a few concessions, like letting her take toys and books with her to bed. Soon everything worked out. Some people would argue that, indeed, Lisa needed more sleep. But at that time, our request was made more for our sake than for hers.

If we find ourselves saying, "I want you to do this because I need (or want) it" too often, we're abusing a good thing. We need to save our "selfish" requests for times when we really need them.

While you are evaluating the demands you make on your child, make a similar evaluation of the rules and regulations that you expect him to follow. Developing a trust relationship with your child will *really* pay off. Especially when he gets to be a teen-ager.

The Need for Security

In my vocation you can't go one day without hearing someone say, "He suffers from a lack of security." What does *security* mean? I thought I knew—until I went to a lecture on child abuse about a year ago.

"Many times children who come from homes where child-beating is common have a greater sense of security than those children who come from homes where no child-beating is found," the lecturer said. A wave of conversation rippled through the crowd. Finally, someone in the group raised his hand and asked, "How can that be?"

The lecturer responded, "Abused children know what to

expect." That made sense to me. I began observing children who were considered to be "insecure" and children who were thought to be "secure." After a six-month comparative study, I came up with new guidelines for meeting a child's security needs. It is my opinion that if a child is to be secure, he must (1) know what to expect, (2) know where he stands, and (3) feel safe. Knowing what to expect and knowing where he stands can be a reality for your child only if you are honest and consistent with him. Again, this requires that you be "real."

I think it is important, also, to say that a parent cannot fulfill all of a child's emotional needs. Hopefully, the adults that surround your child—his teachers, coaches, and significant others—will assume some of the load, as will the child's peers.

It's up to us as parents to get our children into situations where they are with people who will help get the job done. We need to make sure that some of the adults and children who surround our children are caring people—capable of loving and respecting them. We also need to see that there are people around our children whom they can trust and feel secure with. Negative relationships do far more harm than they ever do good.

We left a school once because it lacked adults who truly cared for Christopher. That is how serious I consider this to be.

Summary

A. A child has four basic emotional needs:
   1. He must be *loved* (valued). This will be evident as you share your time, efforts, and possessions with him.
   2. He must be *respected*—not for what you want him to be, but for what he is right now.
   3. He must be able to *trust* that the things you want for

him are for his good. This will require an evaluation of what you are demanding from him and the rules and procedures that you expect him to follow.

4. He must feel *secure* by knowing what to expect, knowing where he stands, and feeling safe.

B. See that your child is surrounded by other caring adults and children who will help you meet his emotional needs.

6

"*Mommy, I'm Bored!*"

Meeting a Child's Creative and Intellectual Needs

Guy had been actively involved for over a year in the childrens' program at the church where I was on staff. We had become very good friends. One afternoon, to my surprise, his mother dropped by my office to talk to me about a problem Guy was having at school.

"We're at the end of our rope with Guy," she began. "We've tried everything to help him achieve at school, but nothing seems to work. Every year his grades get worse. I found his report card—the one he had supposedly lost—hidden in the top of his closet. And no wonder! The two highest grades on it were C's—one in physical education and one in math. His teacher has had it, too. She is going to recommend that he be retained if his grades do not improve radically by the end of the year."

I was shocked! This did not sound like the Guy that I knew!

Mrs. Stanley continued: "Guy likes you very much. We think he will listen to you. Would you please talk to him? Maybe you could find out what his problem is."

I made a visit to Guy's home one day after he got home from school. I found him in the backyard playing in the most magnificent treehouse I had ever seen. It was a three-tiered house, equipped with a hand-operated but extremely safe elevator, running water for each level, an ice box securely anchored to the second level, a radio, and storage space. I was so impressed that I had difficulty talking about anything else.

The following dialogue was taken from a tape recording that was made (with Guy's permission) of our session together.

JOY: Golly, that sure is a fabulous treehouse!

GUY: Thanks!

JOY: Did you build it yourself?

GUY: Well, sort of. But not really.

JOY: What do you mean?

GUY: Well, I didn't really build it myself, but it was all my idea.

JOY: Oh? Who actually built it?

GUY: Some bigger guys who live a couple of streets away.

JOY: That was a pretty nice thing for them to do!

GUY: Not really. I paid them for it!

JOY: You did? Where did you get the money?

GUY: From avocados.

JOY: What?

GUY: See those avocado trees out in the yard? My mom made me pick up all the avocados that fell on the ground. One day I asked my dad if I could have the avocados that I picked up. He didn't care. No one in our family liked to eat them, so they just rotted on the ground. That's why I had to pick them up. I sold all the avocados and got enough money to build the treehouse.

Joy: *You* sold the avocados to get enough money to build the treehouse?

Guy: Oh, no. I got some kids to help me!

Joy: How did you manage to do that?

Guy: I told them that they could be the first members of my treehouse club if they sold enough avocados. (Guy starts to laugh.) Julie—that's one of the treehouse members—sorta got in trouble. We were selling the avocados at the Hub Shopping Center and Julie was arrested—well, not really, but sort of. We weren't supposed to sell anything without a permit.

Joy: Did you get enough money to buy all of the wood for the treehouse?

Guy: In a way. But most of it I got for free.

Joy: Who gave you free wood?

Guy: Some of it we got when the Buckners tore down Shannon's bedroom to make it bigger, but most of it we got from Ken. He's the treehouse vice-president.

Joy: Where did he get the wood?

Guy: His dad is a carpenter. Ken got the wood from his dad for doing chores around the house. He didn't have to sell any avocados and he got to be vice-president because he got the wood.

Joy: Well, where did all the money go?

Guy: We paid the guys who built the treehouse $10 each. There were three of them. But I told them what I wanted.

Joy: How is the treehouse club going now?

Guy: Oh, fine, I guess. But I want to start a new club, a skateboard club.

Joy: Oh? How will you get your skateboards? Where will you get the money for them?

(Guy disappears for a moment and then returns with a large, rather worn, accountant's ledger book. The book contains a complete and accurate record of every penny that had ever been spent.)

GUY: We charge the kids in the neighborhood 25¢ a day to play in the treehouse. Sometimes we give shows and parties in the treehouse for money. And then there's other things we do.

JOY: Unbelievable!

(This ended our conversation about the treehouse. We talked about several other things, and then I asked him a question.)

JOY: Guy, what do you think you do best?

GUY: Not really anything . . . I really don't get very good grades. I can't draw and . . .

JOY: Think hard!

GUY: Well, I don't like sports and I don't like music. Really, I'm not good at anything. Is that why you came to my house to talk to me? Are you disappointed in me, too?

Let me end this story by saying that Guy's parents finally transferred him to a school where children like Guy were valued, challenged, and given an opportunity to learn through a highly individualized program of instruction. The last I heard, Guy was on his way to conquering the world!

In regard to Guy's intellectual abilities, it was not that Guy was not *able* to perform at school, it was that he was not *motivated*. Realizing this, I would be inclined to feel that Guy's report card was *not* as much a reflection on him as it was on the system. Failure in school is too often blamed on the child, and unjustly so. It is the responsibility of parents and teachers to see that children are not given subject matter that they are not developmentally ready to handle. It is also the responsibility of the teachers to motivate children to learn the subject matter that they are ready for. Readiness is often demonstrated by the questions the child asks, the things he is curious about or things he wants to understand. When teachers fill out report cards they are, in many ways, grading themselves!

The Intellectual Cycle

In order to see that a child's intellectual needs are met, one must understand what I call the "intellectual cycle." The intellectual cycle usually begins with curiosity, questions, or the desire to understand. It then moves on to exploration and exploration leads to discovery. Discovery then brings about reinforcement (affirmation). It goes something like this:

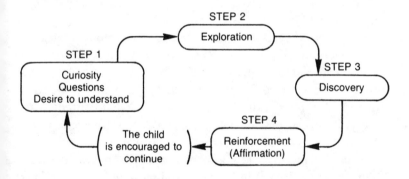

Leaving out any one of the steps makes the intellectual cycle incomplete and inhibits intellectual growth (learning). It also frustrates the child.

In Guy's situation, he did not get past step one. The subject matter being offered at school was nothing that stimulated his curiosity or his desire to understand. The cycle was incomplete and Guy experienced very little intellectual growth.

Not all children get stopped at step one. For example,

most toddlers, born with tons of curiosity, questions, and the desire to understand, move quickly to step two. They want to explore everything they can get their hands on, but all too often they're "cut off at the pass" with a "No, No!" or a "Don't touch!" or a smack on the bottom. They never reach the discovery phase, the cycle is incomplete and the child becomes frustrated.

There are older children who also can't make it past step two or step three because their natural curiosity and questioning is not valued. They wonder "How high is the sky?" or "Why is the grass green?" but their questions may not be a part of the standard school curriculum and so they are never given the time or the tools with which to explore and discover. Again the cycle is broken and frustration results.

Hopefully, sometimes a child is able to make it past steps one, two and three to step four. "Reinforcement" occurs when the child receives some kind of affirmation because of a discovery he has made. Reinforcement can be internal (the sheer pleasure of discovering something new) or external (approval and appreciation by others of the discovery). At first, children seem to be somewhat content with internal affirmation, but as they get older and become more and more socialized, they seem to require more and more external affirmation. The aim of most parents and teachers should be to help a child become self-motivated (less reliant on external reinforcement).

The intellectual cycle can be brought on by parents or teachers who stimulate a child's curiosity and his desire to understand. Parents and teachers can also bring on the intellectual cycle by providing the necessary "tools" for exploration and discovery. However, some of the time the intellectual cycle can occur for a child without the aid of an adult. My observation of Ronnie, a twenty-four-month-old dynamo, is a good example of what I mean. The following account is taken from notes I made while observing him at a park.

Ronnie sees a ball, runs over to it, picks it up and throws it at random. The ball hits the steps of a nearby climbing toy and bounces back at him. He is absolutely thrilled! He gets the ball and this time he purposely throws it at the steps. The ball bounces back toward him and he expresses a great deal of delight. He repeats this activity seven more times. After the seventh time, he takes the ball over to the slide and throws it at that. The ball bounces back. Ronnie repeats this activity six times. The sixth time, he throws the ball farther up the slide and, as it rolls down the slide and onto the sand, he picks it up. He walks up the face of the slide, holding the ball in one hand and balancing himself with the other. When he gets to the top of the slide, he extends his legs, spreads them apart and rolls the ball down the slide, and then slides down after it. He then retrieves the ball from the sand and repeats the entire activity several times. He is going up the slide with the ball a fourth time when his mother stops him, takes him off the slide and ties his shoe laces. After this, he returns to the slide and repeats the whole thing one more time. He then leaves the slide and runs to the merry-go-round and throws the ball at it. The ball rolls back to him and he picks it up and throws it at a post. When the ball bounces off the post, he picks it up and throws it again at the post. This time the ball misses the post and rolls down some steps and into some bushes. Ronnie crawls into the bushes and retrieves the ball, but accidentally drops it. The ball rolls back into the bushes and, once again, he goes after it. Soon he surfaces holding the ball with both hands. He hurries up the steps, carrying the ball with one hand. At the top of the steps, he turns around and rolls the ball back down the steps. The ball again rolls into the bushes and again he goes after it. After about thirty seconds, he comes out of the bushes, holding the ball with both hands. He climbs up the steps again and runs over to the merry-go-round and tosses the ball onto it. It rolls off the merry-go-round, but he does not go after it. His mother calls out to him from where she is sitting, "Do you want to ride, Ronnie?" Ronnie answers by saying in a loud voice, "All right!"

Here the intellectual cycle was set into motion when Ronnie threw the ball and it accidentally hit the steps of the climbing toy. He became curious and may have asked himself, "What happened? How did it happen? Can it happen again?" Exploration began when he started purposely throwing the ball at the steps. When he discovered that the same thing would happen every time, he began exploring with the ball in other ways by throwing it at different objects. The thrill of discovery was Ronnie's reinforcement. The entire intellectual cycle repeated itself several times in a matter of minutes without adult intervention or assistance. Ronnie, through the normal functioning of the intellectual cycle, educated himself!

The Creativity Cycle

The "creativity cycle" is very similar to the intellectual cycle. It is a four-step cycle and begins with the desire to create something. Step two is the process of creating, or the process of bringing something into existence that has never existed before. The third step happens when the creation has been completed; the fourth step occurs when the creation has been accepted. Sometimes I find that parents understand it better when I explain the cycle using these words: step one = "wanting to," step two = "doing it," step three = "having it," and step four = "accepting it." On a chart it would look something like this:

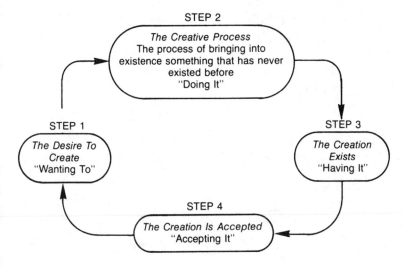

Again, all four steps must take place before the cycle is complete. An example of a completed process would be the child who is given a blank sheet of paper and a box of crayons. Immediately, he wants to color a picture on the paper (step one: "wanting to"). With the crayons he colors a picture on the paper (step two: "doing it"). When he is finished, he has a picture of, say, a dinosaur (step three: "having it"). Hopefully, he will be pleased with what he has drawn (step four: "accepting it"). Because he is pleased with his work, he will feel confident enough to begin the cycle again. If he does not accept his creation, or if someone else doesn't accept it, he will be hesitant to try again.

Most of us have, at one time or another, had the pleasure of experiencing the completed creativity cycle. Unfortunately for many children, this experience does not happen often enough. One reason for this can be found in this story.

The Little Girl with Magical Powers

Once upon a time
a long time ago

there lived a little girl
a very special girl
a
   girl
     with
       magical
         powers

The little girl would look up into the sky
and while others only saw clouds
she could see
the fairyland there
with all of the fairies busy at work and play
and she knew
that the fairyland was a very secret place
a place that only she could see
she
   had
     such
       magical
         powers

The little girl would find a rock
and while others saw that the rock
was nothing special
she could see
the tiny flecks of silver and gold
that were embedded in the surface of the rock
and she knew
all about the precious diamond
that was buried deep inside
she
   had
     such
       magical
         powers

The little girl would see a tiny bug
and while others thought the bug
was only an insect
she could see
that the bug was a funny little character
with a personality and feelings
and she knew
that the bug could talk his own special language
and think his own special thoughts
she
   had
      such
         magical
            powers

The little girl could take an old paper bag
and while others thought
that the bag was just another paper bag
she could make
a puppet, a purse, a doll
a basket or a hat
and she knew
that the paper bag could be
anything she wanted it to be because
she
   had
      such
         magical
            powers

Every day
the little girl grew
until she was big enough
to go to school

One day during recess
the little girl found a quiet spot
on the grassy playground and lay down.

She was watching the fairies busily at work
in their fairyland.
"What are you looking at?" a friend asked.
"The fairies in fairyland," the little girl said.
The friend looked at the clouds and then
looked at the little girl
"Those aren't fairies," he said, "Those
are only clouds."
"Oh," thought the little girl
and so she learned that clouds were only clouds.

Then one day during show-and-tell
the little girl shared her favorite rock.
"This rock is a special rock" she said
"It's covered with gold and silver
and it has a diamond inside."
The teacher came closer and examined the rock.
"That's not gold and silver," she said.
"That's only iron pyrate and mica."
"Oh," thought the little girl.
And so she learned that the sparkles in her rock
were only iron pyrate and mica.

Then one day on her way to school
the little girl found a small red ladybug.
She gently picked up the bug and said
"How are you today?"
"That bug can't talk," jeered one of her friends.
"He's only a bug, and bugs can't talk."
"Oh," thought the little girl.
And she learned that bugs were only bugs.

Then one day after lunch
the little girl emptied her lunch bag
and placed it on her hand.
"How are you today?" the girl asked the bag
that had become a puppet.

The teacher on lunch duty interrupted
"Who are you talking to?"
"My friend," the little girl answered,
pointing to the paper bag.
"That's nothing but a paper bag," the teacher said.
"Oh," said the little girl.
And she learned that paper bags could only be
paper bags.

As the little girl continued to grow
she learned many things.
She learned as all intelligent people do
that things are only what they really are.

And she also learned that
she was just an ordinary girl
with
   no
      magical
       powers.

The people in this story blocked the completion of the creativity cycle by inhibiting the creative process (step two: "doing it"). Another way in which adults prevent the cycle from becoming complete is by not accepting a child's creation (step four: "accepting it").

For too long, creativity has been limited to the fine arts. "If you can draw pictures, write songs, stories or poetry, or choreograph dances, you are creative. But if you do not have gifts or talents in these areas, you aren't creative." Everywhere I go, people tell me, "I never was, and probably never will be creative!" My response to them is, "Everyone is creative—or has had, at one time, the potential of being creative."

To create means to bring into existence something that has never existed before. A creation can be anything!

Lisa brought something into existence recently when she

went on a field trip to the beach with her preschool class. The children were watching a man trying to encourage his dog into the water. The dog was afraid and resisted the man's coaxing. One of the children commented, "I wonder what that dog's name is?" to which Lisa replied, "Chicken of the sea!" The humorous thought that Lisa had created was accepted with laughter.

Creativity can be expressed in many ways. Bringing organization into existence where chaos once prevailed is creative. Bringing a relationship into existence that did not exist before (making friends) is creative. Making money, making "deals," making peace, problem solving are all creative.

We were all born with the ability to create. You were given gifts to enable you to be creative—just as I was. You, along with everyone else, are "gifted."

Discovering your gifts, accepting them and appreciating them comprise the first step in becoming a creative person. This is also true for your child.

How does one go about discovering his gifts? Begin with what you enjoy doing. A real "gift" is not only that which you're good at, but it's also something which you enjoy doing.

A mother once asked me, "Could you talk to Danny and encourage him to play the piano? He wants to stop taking piano and take drum lessons instead. He has been bugging me about it for the last two years. I refuse to let him quit his piano lessons because it's obvious that he's a gifted pianist!" "If he really were a gifted pianist," I answered, "he would *want* to play the piano."

Danny's mother was doing what so many of us do. We confuse gifts with abilities and skills. A child may have the ability or skill to do something, but unless the ability or skill is accompanied by desire, it is not a true gift.

It is in the creation of our gifts that we can see the cleverness of God. He created us with gifts and, to make sure that they are used, he created us with the desire to use them.

Many of us have hidden gifts. Gifts become hidden when we discover early in life that they do not fit into the "acceptable gift" category. Gifts that are being squelched by non-use cause a great deal of frustration and anxiety. In order to avoid this, parents need to help their children discover and use their true gifts.

This will be hard for those parents who have difficulty accepting their child's true gifts when they really want their child to have gifts in other areas instead. It has been hard for me to accept the fact that my children do not have certain gifts, but I shape up when I remind myself that Christopher and Lisa will never function at their maximum capacity until they are allowed to be themselves through the development and use of their gifts.

Providing the Environment

Parents and teachers can stimulate a child's intellectual growth and creativity by seeing that his environment allows the intellectual and creative cycle to happen. I encourage adults to see that a child's environment includes such materials, supplies, books, records, toys, and equipment that, in addition to having educational potential, also have these qualities:

1. *Versatility.* The things that are provided for children should have more than one use. This not only promotes creative thinking, but also insures that the article will be used more than one time. Nothing is worse than buying a toy for a child and having it discarded after using it only once.

2. *Durability.* Anything a child uses receives a "work-out." Avoid disappointments and upsets by providing things that do not break easily.

3. *Workability.* Nothing is more frustrating than something that does not work either because it is broken or because it is "fake." Plastic hammers that do not hammer and plastic lipstick that is not real are frustrating. Make sure that toys and equipment are in good repair and that they do what they are supposed to do.

4. *Independence.* Do not provide things for children that require a lot of adult supervision to use. The more that children do on their own, the more valid their experiences will be. Make sure to provide children with things they are physically and mentally ready to handle. If you give them things that are beyond their abilities, they are likely to fail.

5. *Safety.* For your peace of mind and your child's safety, make sure that he is surrounded with safe toys and equipment.

6. *Attractiveness.* Remember to provide things that are attractive to the child. If he is not attracted to the object, it is less likely that he will use it.

Also, make sure that there is a variety of things for your child to do and that some of those things encourage him to play with other children. Some toys are designed to be shared. A few of these are good to have.

Providing a stimulating environment for the child is not "pushing" him. There is a difference between "motivating" a child and "pushing" him. When a child is pushed, he is not given an option as to whether or not he wants to do something. I advocate motivating children (encouraging them) instead of pushing (forcing) them.

Meeting a child's intellectual and creative needs is as much for the parents' sake as it is for him. Like the rattlesnake's rattle, the "Mommy, I'm bored!" cry serves as a warning that something bad could happen. Unfulfilled creative and intellectual needs are one of the most common causes of misbehavior.

One time in a small group of fourth, fifth, and sixth grade boys, I held up a picture of some boys vandalizing a stop sign by spray-painting it. When I asked the boys to comment, they offered the following observations:

> KEITH: They are going to get it!
> JOY: Why?
> KEITH: Because they're not s'posed to do it.

JOY: Why?

KEITH: I don't know why; I just know they are going to get it!

JOY: Why do you think they are doing it?

ROBERT: Because they have nothing else to do!

JOY: Are they bored?

THE GROUP: Yes!

JOY: Have you ever been bored?

THE GROUP: Yes.

JOY: What do you do about it?

ANDY: I find something to do—and most of the time I guess it's bad!

Summary

The intellectual cycle is as follows.

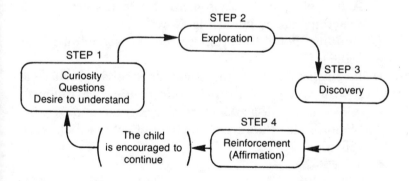

Leaving out any one of these steps makes the intellectual cycle incomplete and inhibits intellectual growth (learning). It also frustrates the child.

The creative cycle is as follows.

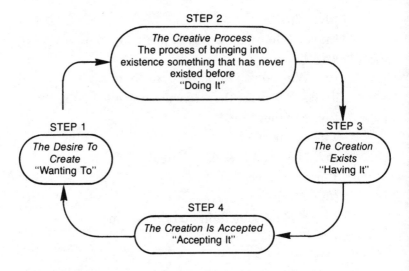

STEP 2

The Creative Process
The process of bringing into
existence something that has never
existed before
"Doing It"

STEP 1

*The Desire To
Create*
"Wanting To"

STEP 3

*The Creation
Exists*
"Having It"

STEP 4

The Creation Is Accepted
"Accepting It"

All four steps must occur in order to complete the cycle.

A. To create means to bring into existence something that has never existed before. Creativity can be expressed in many ways.

B. A true gift is not only something one is good at, it is something one enjoys doing as well.

C. Children should be encouraged to discover and use their "true gifts."

D. Parents and teachers can stimulate a child's intellectual growth and creativity by seeing that his environment allows the intellectual and creative cycles to come to completion. The child's environment should include such things that are

1. versatile,
2. durable,
3. workable,
4. independent,
5. safe,
6. attractive.

E. There should be a variety of things, some of which should encourage sharing.
F. There is a difference between "pushing" and "motivating"...
    1. Pushing is forcing.
    2. Motivating is encouraging.
G. Unfulfilled intellectual and creative needs are oftentimes the cause of misbehavior.

7

The Bible ... Rated "R"

Meeting a Child's Spiritual Needs

When Christopher was three years old, my husband, Bruce, took him on a Saturday outing to the Big Slide. Returning home from the trip, Christopher bounded out of the car and ran into the house yelling at the top of his lungs. "Mom! I just saw a slide that was bigger than God!" At three years of age, Chris had already begun to formulate in his mind what he thought God was like.

Believing in God is not a difficult thing for children. My experience in dealing with children has led me to believe that children are born with three basic spiritual needs. The first need is to know about God, the second is to have a relationship with God, and the third need is to please God.

I feel that a child's need to know about and believe in God is evidenced by his tendency toward and acceptance of fictional characters like Santa Claus, the Easter Bunny, fairies, etc. All of these characters have God-like qualities: they are wise, just, kind, generous, capable of servicing the entire world—all at the same time, and they live in mystical places that can't be pinpointed on a map.

If it is true that children have a need to know about and believe in God, how do parents go about seeing that this need is met?

For years parents have depended upon the church to meet their children's spiritual needs. Has this approach been effective? During the last year I have made an attempt to answer this question for myself by visiting all kinds of churches and talking to all kinds of people who have an opinion on the subject.

Some time ago I visited a sixth grade Sunday school class. The tension in the classroom was incredible. I felt it immediately when I entered the room. Isolated in the farthest corner of the classroom was a girl, defiantly sitting in a chair and leaning against the wall. Her arms were folded in rebellion, and she angrily stared at the teacher.

"Julie does not know how to listen," the teacher told me, "and until she can learn how, we thought she might be better off away from the rest of the group." She was addressing me, but in tones loud enough for everyone to hear.

I had come to this particular church to observe "one of the better Sunday school programs" in our area. I was disappointed to find that this program, like other programs I had recently observed in other churches, was unbelievably identical to the outdated Sunday school program that I had experienced some twenty-five years ago as a child.

The teacher began. "Let's see if we can remember what we talked about last week." Immediately, Julie shouted out, "the ten plagues!" Refusing to acknowledge Julie, the teacher went on. "Can anyone tell us something about the ten plagues?" Julie began spieling out the exact name of each plague, and in proper chronological order. Halfway through the list, the teacher interrupted: "No one asked you to comment, Julie!" It was as though the teacher had pushed Julie's "Tell us how you really feel" button. Julie jumped to her feet and shouted, "It's too bad no one asked me to comment! If they did, I'd tell them just how sick I am of listening to the same old stories over and over again. Can't we *talk* about something else? Can't we *do* something else?"

"Well, Julie, it's obvious that you aren't happy in our class," the teacher responded. "Perhaps you would be better off not staying here with us." Fighting back the tears, Julie started toward the door. She glanced despairingly at her peers who sat helplessly in their seats. Within a few seconds she was out of the room and it was quiet again. The class went on.

Julie's problem was not that she did not know how to listen. On the contrary, listening was all she had been doing in Sunday school and she was sick of it.

She, along with thousands of children all over the United States, is the victim of a *non*-do-it-yourself approach to Christian education. Learning about God for too many children is a boring experience that "happens" to them on Sunday morning. Have you ever wondered how children view their church experience?

In a recent survey, many children from various kinds of church experiences were asked these three questions: tell us about church, what is it? and how do you feel about it? The results were devastating. The following responses are typical of attitudes expressed by most of the children interviewed:

"Church is a place where you have to dress up and wear squeaky shoes . . . UGH!"

"Church is where my mom and dad make me go on Sundays."

"At church, they just talk, talk, talk."

"I like church medium." Then, in a whisper, "Well, really not even medium, but I don't want to hurt God's feelings."

"Church was more fun for kids when Jesus was on earth, because he let them have class outside and they sat on his lap!"

"I'd rather watch 'Wonderama' (a secular Sunday-morning TV program for children) than go to church anytime!"

"One time I liked church when our teacher let us help teach the lesson."

"I guess I can stand it for a while. I just keep telling myself that someday I'll be big enough to not go."

In another survey, a total of 192 children from first to sixth grades were asked, "Why do you go to Sunday school?" Of this number, 62 said "I don't know," 14 said it was because they liked it (but only a few of them were able to say *why* they liked it), 99 of the children said that it was because their parents made them go, and 17 said that they went to Sunday school because they didn't want to go to hell.

The spiritual damage done to children in the church during the first twelve years of their lives is oftentimes irreparable. They usually begin leaving the church at about the age of thirteen. Too often, their rejection of the church becomes a rejection of God as well. There's got to be a way of preventing these thirteen-year-olds from saying "I've had it!"

Our "prevention program" should begin with a reevaluation of how parents are going about the process of meeting their children's spiritual needs. "Dumping kids off" at church on Sunday morning and expecting the church to do the job is obviously not acceptable. Seeing that the child's spiritual needs are met is the direct responsibility of the parents. A child's church experience should merely be a supplement to what is happening in the home. If "supplementary" church experiences are used, they should be under the constant scrutiny of the parents to make sure that what the child is experiencing at church is consistent with what he is learning at home.

Following the evaluation of how our child's spiritual needs are being met, we should reevaluate *what* we are teaching our child about God and *how* we are going about it. The time has come for the Christian community to take advantage of the years of research and study done by secular child developmentalists and educators. If we are to teach children about God, it is imperative that we discover *how* children learn and *what* they are capable of learning.

A knowledge of these two facts would completely revolutionize Christian educational experiences for children. The Sunday school and the home curriculum would be an "experience" curriculum because parents and teachers would realize that children learn most from doing and least from listening. It would be an enjoyable curriculum because parents and teachers would know that a child's play is his greatest educational tool. Biblical concepts (the meaning of the Bible) would receive more attention than biblical facts because the parents and teachers would understand that biblical facts are historical facts and children have a tremendously hard time implementing historical facts into their daily living.

Recently, I was asked to evaluate a set of curriculum goals that a Christian education committee had established for their first- through-sixth-graders. The proposal came to me in the form of a forty-seven-page typewritten report. The comprehensive study that was advocated included two complete surveys of the Bible (accompanied by the memorization of appropriate biblical facts), the memorization of 312 Scripture verses, exposure to all sorts of church doctrines (including such "heavies" as predestination and eternal security), and a "partridge in a pear tree"! When the chairman of the Christian education committee was asked to state the reasons for initiating the proposal, he replied, "We've learned that we're only going to have these children for twelve years, and we're committing ourselves to getting them through the Bible, if it's the last thing we do!"

Too often we are so busy "getting them through the Bible" that they end up missing its message.

One Sunday morning I was watching a group of third grade children play a memory verse game. The object of the game was to see who could be the first to run to the center of the room and recite a given memory verse. The teacher called out a reference: "Matthew 7:12!" Three children ran to the center of the room and collided. The fight that developed took both the teacher and I several minutes to break up. When things had calmed down, it was decided that each child would be given the opportunity to say the verse. I found it interesting that all three of the children could recite the verse perfectly, but I seriously questioned whether or not they knew what the words they rattled off meant.

I believe that our preoccupation with biblical *facts* rather than biblical *concepts* is where we miss the boat. To me, the Christian faith is based upon a set of simple biblical concepts. As one "grows in the faith," he may gather up supportive facts for those concepts, but the concepts never change. The older one gets, the more supportive facts he seems to require in order to continue believing in the simple concepts. On the other hand, children will accept the concepts with very little explanation.

In short, adults may enjoy *Chicken Souffle,* but kids will choose hot dogs every time. When you deal with children, it's best to keep it simple!

Over the last thirteen years I've come up with a list of the simple biblical concepts which I feel children can understand, assimilate and apply. There are a million ways to teach these concepts: I encourage the use of experiences involving the senses, field trips, multi-media, drama, art, music, rhythm, body movement, and so on. I feel that Bible stories and facts should be used only if and when they apply. "Stretching" a Bible story to teach a biblical concept is not a good procedure.

Here is a list of simple biblical concepts that I believe children can handle:

God

GOD IS REAL. There may come a time when your child questions whether or not God is real. It would likely occur about the same time that he discovers that Santa Claus is, in fact, mom and dad. Once I had a disillusioned child tell me, "My parents told me that Santa Claus was real and I found out that he wasn't. They didn't tell me the truth about him—how do I know they're telling me the truth about God?" It is this kind of question that frightens many parents into "throwing the baby out with the bath." They do not allow their child to believe in any imaginary characters because they fear that it will hinder him from believing in God. Some parents also feel that Santa Claus, the Easter Bunny, fairies, etc., would detract from the child's relationship with God.

I believe that imaginary characters are not only a vital part of a child's heritage and cultural experience, but a delightful part of growing up. God is much too secure to be threatened by Santa Claus! In the long run, as your child grows older, he will find far more meaning in his relationship with God than he ever did with any of his imaginary friends.

How, then, does a parent handle all of this? From the very beginning, help your child make the distinction between "imaginary" and "real." Imaginary characters depend on the imagination for their existence. Before they can exist, they have to be imagined. Spiritual beings are different. The spiritual world is a real world, even though we can't see it. I often illustrate this point by using some room deodorant. You may not be able to see it, but your other senses tell you that it's there. You can't see God, but your spiritual sense will tell you that he is real. If a person never imagined or thought of God, it wouldn't make any difference. God would still exist; his existence is not dependent on thoughts or imaginations.

As for the idea that holiday characters like Santa Claus and the Easter Bunny conflict with the "true meaning" of the holidays, check this out before you make any snap judgments. Many of our secular holiday symbols have religious beginnings and meanings. For example, the Easter egg to early Christians was symbolic of the "new life" found in Christ. The Easter Bunny symbolized fertility and was to be an example to Christians who were to procreate the faith. A lot of the holiday symbols have religious meanings. If you are interested, you can find lots of fascinating material in the encyclopedia.

If you are unable to find religious meanings for all of the holiday customs and traditions, don't fret. Remember, your child can be many things in addition to being a Christian. He has a heritage and a culture that he should be proud of, too. Many of our customs cannot be justified religiously, but culturally they can.

Parents who deprive their children of fun and exciting cultural experiences in the name of Christianity do them an injustice. Subconsciously, the child begins to think, "I don't know much about Christianity, but I know I don't like it. Being a Christian means missing out on all the fun!" On the contrary, God delights in our enjoyment of life.

A good balance of meaningful religious experiences and practical cultural experiences makes a healthy, well-rounded child.

God is perfect. He never makes mistakes. We shall talk more about this when we get to the chapter that deals with trauma.

God is love. The Scriptures tell us that we can know who God is because he is love.

God is in control. This concept is a great one to tuck away and bring out on a "rainy day" when everything appears to be falling apart. It's neat to have the assurance that God is always in control.

God created the whole universe, including man. Please don't make an issue out of evolution. Maybe God created the earth, plants, and animals via the evolutionary process and maybe he didn't. The important thing is that *God* created the world—and that's pretty fantastic! Too often, children are caught in the middle of a debate between their parents and their teachers over the topic of evolution and the only one that *really* loses is the child. Also, as a corollary of God's creating the world is the concept that only God can create life.

God loves man and continually tries to communicate with him.

It was Sunday evening and I was sitting on the couch with Christopher and Lisa watching TV. On the way out the door, Bruce had managed to give me a "you really ought to be going to church with me!" look. I knew he was disappointed in me for not going with him, but at this stage of the game, I really didn't care. The last few months of my life had been inundated with trauma and I felt whipped.

Well-meaning friends had added to my depression by suggesting that "maybe there was sin in my life and God was punishing me for it." Advice ranged from "you need to fast for a week" to "begin on page one of the Bible and keep reading until you come across something that leaps out at you!" Read! I thought to myself, I can't even think! Besides, because of everything that had happened, God and I weren't on very good speaking terms!

I was so mentally and emotionally beat that I, without realizing it, had relinquished my turn to choose the TV program to Christopher and Lisa. Before I knew what was happening, Tinker Bell had waved her magic wand across the TV screen and "The Wonderful World of Disney" had begun.

The Disney movie that night was a real tear-jerker. It was about an Indian girl who had entered her horse in a race to determine whether or not her tribe would be able to keep their land. For weeks she put the horse through an extremely arduous training program, forcing him to achieve almost impossible feats. When the day of the race came, the horse was ready and won with flying colors and everyone lived happily ever after.

When the movie was over and all three of us sat on the couch with tears streaming down our cheeks. Chris's and Lisa's tears were tears of joy for the horse and the Indian girl. Mine weren't. God had spoken to me through that simple Disney movie. I felt as though he had told me that I was in training for a big race—a race that I would someday win if I could somehow survive the rigors of the training program. The traumas that I had suffered were going to make me a stronger person.

God spoke to me . . . not through prayer and Scripture reading, but through a common, everyday occurrence. He reached out to me and met me where I was.

Although the Bible is a tremendous source from which God communicates to man, it scares me to think that we would limit him to that. God is clever and creative. He can and will use whatever we are tuned in to in order to communicate with us. God loves us and will continually, through a variety of ways, strive to communicate his love and purpose for our lives.

It is the same for our child. We need to help him to turn on and tune in to God through his life experiences.

GOD WANTS US TO LOVE AND RESPECT HIM, ourselves and others. Before we move into the simple concepts about Jesus, I'd like to share with you the exact story I tell children when they ask questions like, "How could Jesus be God?" and "Why did they kill Jesus?" Please remember that this story has been simplified and translated into words and concepts that children can understand and assimilate.

A long time ago, before Jesus was born, whenever a person would do something wrong, he would kill an animal to prove to God that he was really sorry for his mistake. Some people think that God *wanted* those people to do this for *his* sake. I don't agree. I think that God was crushed whenever a person made a mistake—not because of what it did to him, but because of what it did to the person. God knew that the person would feel guilty. He also knew that "feeling guilty" could do terrible things to him. God had made that person and he loved him very much. He didn't want him to be hurt, so he gave him a way to "make up" for his mistake so that he could accept God's forgiveness and forget it!

I've made a lot of mistakes in my time and I've really been sorry for them, but I've never killed an animal to prove that I was sorry. Do you know why? It's because I know something that the people who lived before Jesus was born did not know. I know all about God's forgiveness. How do I know about God's forgiveness?

By reading about Jesus in the Bible. You see, Jesus was God.

The world was quite a few years old by the time God made his personal visit to the earth. He had been watching his people hating, fighting and doing all kinds of horrible things to hurt one another. God felt terrible! After all, he had made those people and there they were—destroying one another! (Have you ever had someone destroy something you made? It's pretty awful, isn't it?)

God had been trying to tell the people to "shape up!" by talking to the few people who would listen to him (people like Moses, Samuel, Isaiah, and others). These prophets—that's what they were called—tried to tell the people what God was telling them, but the message just wasn't getting through! If I want the job done right, God said to himself, I'll just have to do it myself! So he made himself into a man and came to earth so that he could talk to the people in person, face to face! God came to the earth just like all of us did—he was born. You know that story, so I'll just get on with my story.

Jesus—that was God's name while he was here on earth—told everyone that they were to love God, love themselves, and love each other, and then he showed them how to do it by doing it himself. He was perfect. He never made a mistake. (That's how I know that Jesus was God, because only God is perfect!)

Some people couldn't stand Jesus. I think they were jealous of him because they couldn't be perfect like he was. But, for whatever their reasons, they decided to do something that I feel was totally unforgivable! One day they humiliated Jesus by saying all kinds of mean things to him and then they beat him up. As though that wasn't enough, they finally killed him. They didn't have any reason to hurt him; he had never done anything wrong to them or to anyone else. As far as I'm concerned, I think they should never have been forgiven, but, you see, I'm not God! Jesus was. And do you know what he did? He forgave them because, as he put it, "They didn't know what they were doing."

Do you know what we can learn from Jesus' death?

There is nothing worse that anyone can do to a person than to kill him. The people who killed Jesus did the worst possible thing to him, but he still forgave them.

By God becoming a man and going through what he did, he showed us that no matter how bad the mistakes are that we make, *nothing* is too bad for God to forgive. If we are really sorry for our mistakes, God will forgive us. If we accept his forgiveness, we do not have to feel guilty.

Continuing, then, with the simple biblical concepts we discussed earlier in this chapter:

Jesus

JESUS WAS GOD.
JESUS LIVED:
So that man could understand God better.
To show how God wanted man to live.
JESUS DIED TO TEACH MAN ABOUT GOD'S FORGIVENESS.
JESUS ROSE FROM THE DEAD TO SHOW MAN THAT:
God has power over death.
There is another life after death.

The Holy Spirit—is God in the world today

The Bible

THE MESSAGE CONTAINED IN THE BIBLE IS GOD'S MESSAGE TO MAN.
GOD'S MESSAGE IS TRUE.
GOD'S MESSAGE IS RELEVANT TO EVERY MAN.

When parents ask me why I say that the Bible is "Rated R," I tell them that the Bible is a book which was written by adults for adults. Many portions of the Bible are not suitable for children to read. For this reason, I consider the Bible to be "Rated R." It is up to knowledgable adults to glean from the Bible the important concepts and then teach them to the children in a way that will be understandable to them.

Because the Bible is an adult's book, many children do not enjoy reading it. I strongly feel that they should never be made to believe that their lack of interest in the Bible means that they are not interested in God. Neither should they be made to feel that if they do not understand the Bible, God cannot talk to them. God can—and does—speak to children in many different ways.

The Church

ALL OF THE FOLLOWERS OF GOD TOGETHER MAKE THE CHURCH.

This really throws the kids. They think the church is a building. When teaching Sunday school, I teach this concept by taking the children to the park during the regular Sunday school hour. Inevitably, someone will ask, "Aren't we going to church today?" My answer: "We *are* the church. We're taking the church to the park!"

GOD WANTS ALL OF HIS FOLLOWERS TO COME TOGETHER SO THEY CAN:

worship him,
learn more about him,
serve him.

GOD ALSO WANTS HIS FOLLOWERS TO:

love each other and help each other,
tell other people about him so that they will be followers of God, too.

Man

EACH MAN IS A UNIQUE INDIVIDUAL, created by God for a special purpose.

MAN IS FREE TO MAKE HIS OWN DECISIONS.

MAN IS NOT PERFECT. Sometimes he chooses to do wrong.

His wrong doings are never too bad for God to forgive. But, because God loves man, he allows him to suffer the consequences of his mistakes so that he can learn why he should not do it again. I use this explanation because, all too often, children believe that if they say they are sorry and God forgives them for their mistake, they will not have to suffer the consequences of it. This is not true. But, without guilt, "suffering the consequences" can be a positive experience instead of a negative one.

EVERY MAN NEEDS GOD.

MAN, APART FROM GOD, BECOMES VERY SELF-CENTERED.

I do not believe that being self-centered is necessarily

a bad thing. A certain amount of self-centeredness is essential for man's survival. But when man separates himself from God and God's command to "love your neighbor as yourself," man becomes self-centered to the degree that he begins to demand things for himself at the expense of other people. Self-centeredness becomes wrong when it begins to infringe on the rights of other people.

MAN, WITH GOD, HAS TREMENDOUS POTENTIAL TO ACCOMPLISH GOOD.

Other Subjects

The following are subjects that I never bring up, but if a child does ask about them, I answer them briefly as follows:

HEAVEN—is being with God forever.

HELL—is being separated from God forever. I never use "fire and brimstone" descriptions of hell, just as I never use the "golden street" description of heaven. I feel that these are inaccurate because they are physical descriptions of spiritual realities. Also, scaring or bribing a child into a relationship with God is unfair. A relationship with God is something that one must enter into by choice.

THE DEVIL—is the enemy of God, the evil force that constantly works against God.

Summary

A. Children have three basic spiritual needs:
   1. To know about God.
   2. To have a relationship with him.
   3. To please him.
B. Parents have depended entirely upon the church to meet their child's spiritual needs. This has not worked. Seeing that a child's spiritual needs are met is the direct responsi-

bility of the parent. The church should be used to provide good supplementary experiences for what is being done at home.

C. When teaching a child about God, remember that:
1. Children learn most from doing and least from listening.
2. Play is a good educational tool.
3. Children have difficulty assimilating and utilizing historical facts.

D. Do not complicate Christianity when dealing with children. Keep it simple.

E. Simple biblical concepts to teach children are:

God

GOD IS:
real,
perfect,
love,
in control.

GOD CREATED THE WHOLE UNIVERSE, including man. Only God can create life.

GOD LOVES MAN AND CONTINUALLY TRIES TO COMMUNICATE WITH HIM.

GOD WANTS US TO LOVE AND RESPECT:
him,
ourselves,
others.

Jesus

JESUS WAS GOD.

JESUS LIVED:
so that man could understand God better.
to show how God wanted man to live.

JESUS DIED TO TEACH MAN ABOUT GOD'S FORGIVENESS.

JESUS ROSE FROM THE DEAD TO SHOW MAN THAT:
God has power over death.
There is another life after death.

The Holy Spirit—is God in the world today.

The Bible

THE MESSAGE CONTAINED IN THE BIBLE IS GOD'S MESSAGE TO MAN.

GOD'S MESSAGE IS TRUE.

GOD'S MESSAGE IS RELEVANT TO EVERY MAN.

The Church

ALL OF THE FOLLOWERS OF GOD TOGETHER MAKE THE CHURCH.

GOD WANTS ALL OF HIS FOLLOWERS TO COME TOGETHER SO THAT THEY CAN:

worship him.

learn more about him.

serve him.

GOD ALSO WANTS HIS FOLLOWERS TO:

love each other and help each other.

tell other people about him so that they will be followers of God, too.

Man

EACH MAN IS A UNIQUE INDIVIDUAL, created by God for a special purpose.

MAN IS FREE to make his own decisions.

MAN IS NOT PERFECT. Sometimes he chooses to do wrong. His wrong doings are never too bad for God to forgive. But, because God loves man, he allows him to suffer the consequences of his wrong doing so he can learn not to do it again.

EVERY MAN NEEDS GOD.

MAN, APART FROM GOD, BECOMES VERY SELF-CENTERED.

MAN, WITH GOD, HAS TREMENDOUS POTENTIAL TO ACCOMPLISH GOOD.

8

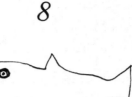

To Spank or Not to Spank
Is Not the Only Question

Discipline

I had been invited to a PTA meeting to speak on the subject of discipline. Upon my arrival, I was met at the door by
a large boisterous woman. "Before I decide to stay for your
lecture, I'd like to know one thing," she told me. "Do you
believe in spankings, or don't you?"

This is a typical response to lectures on discipline. Many
people put parents into two groups: "spankers" and "non-
spankers." Many times "To spank, or not to spank" becomes
the only issue that is dealt with when discipline is discussed.
There is much more to discipline than spanking.

Treating discipline and spanking as though they are one
and the same comes from confusing discipline with punishment. I feel that discipline and punishment are two completely different things. I define *discipline* as "an educational
process whereby a person learns what behavior is or is not
acceptable and why." *Punishment,* on the other hand, is "an
inflicted consequence which a person receives for misbehavior." Discipline may include punishment, but it also includes
a lot more.

While we are defining terms, it may be well to define *misbehavior.* To me, misbehavior is that behavior which:

- Hinders one's relationship with God,
- Harms oneself or hinders one from realizing his potential and achieving his goals,
- Infringes upon the rights of others.

Misbehavior is usually caused by one of four things:

- Unfulfilled needs,
- A lack of understanding (the child does not know better),
- Thinking that the misbehavior is more desirable than acceptable behavior is. Sometimes, children, like adults, misbehave because they feel that they will gain from the act in some way. An aura of fun, excitement, and intrigue seems to surround the "forbidden fruit," the "No-no." Interestingly enough, most children and adults possess a sort of "I'm different—it can't happen to me!" attitude. They honestly feel that they will be exempted from the negative consequences that result from wrong-doing. The combination of these ideas often leads to misbehavior.
- Rebellion. Rebellion happens when a child feels that his right to live his own life is being taken away from him. Rebellion is not always a negative thing. Thank God that our forefathers had enough spunk to rebel against the tax on tea! Beating all of the rebellion out of a child can, in some ways, be detrimental. A child who cannot stand up for his rights as a child will have a difficult time standing up for his rights as an adult. Thus, rebellion is sometimes necessary to protect one's rights. But when one's rebellion begins to infringe upon the rights of others, it becomes misbehavior.

When a child misbehaves, he should be disciplined. There are many ways to discipline a child—all of which work. The skill of disciplining a child comes in knowing what "level" of discipline will effectively correct a specific misbehavior.

Correcting Misbehavior

There are five levels of discipline that are designed to take place *after* misbehavior occurs.

The first level is one which we have been discussing in the last five chapters, namely MEETING THE CHILD'S NEEDS. If a child misbehaves as a result of an unfulfilled need, obviously the most effective method of correction would be to meet the child's need. Three quarters of the behavioral problems can be solved by meeting the child's basic needs.

If a child still misbehaves after you have, to the best of your ability, attempted to see that his basic needs are met, it's time to have a heart-to-heart talk with him. The parent must COMMUNICATE with him. He needs to be told why his (mis) - behavior is unacceptable and what will happen to him if he continues to misbehave. As I mentioned before, many times a child will misbehave because he does not know any better.

If communicating with the child does not correct his misbehavior, it's time to rely on NATURAL CONSEQUENCES to discipline him. Natural consequences are the consequences that result naturally from doing something wrong. This is a concept generally attributed to Rudolph Dreikurs.

Last Halloween my friend's children made quite a "haul" on their Trick or Treat rounds. She warned them that "too much candy will make you sick," but they ignored her advice and proceeded to stuff down at least half of their entire collection. That night they were very sick. Every trip to the bathroom was a reminder that eating as much candy as they did was unacceptable behavior. My friend recently told me that ever since that time she has never had a problem with her children eating too much candy.

Another example of disciplining through natural consequences is in a story told to me by "C. J." a fourth grade student of mine.

C. J.: Well, I remember once when my brother and I found a pack of cigarettes in this place where they were building some new houses.

Joy: Oh? What did you do with them?

C. J.: We took them home and my brother hid them.

JOY: Why did he hide them?

C. J.: Well, my mom and dad (mom especially) told us that we shouldn't smoke.

JOY: Did they tell you why?

C. J.: Yes, they said that it wasn't good for us. They also told us that we might get sick.

JOY: What did you do with the cigarettes?

C. J.: One day we got up enough nerve. We got two of our friends and snuck out into the garage and we smoked the whole pack!

JOY: What happened?

C. J.: Me and my friends got sick. My brother choked real bad and didn't smoke as many as my friends and me. Rick, my brother's friend, didn't want to try it because he saw what happened to us.

JOY: Did you like it?

C. J.: No! It was terrible!

JOY: Did your parents ever find out?

C. J.: Well, one day I told my mom about it.

JOY: What did she say?

C. J.: She said she knew 'cause she had found the pack of cigarettes where my brother had hidden them. I asked her how come she didn't throw them away.

JOY: Why didn't she?

C. J.: She said that she knew that we'd have to learn the hard way about smoking because that's the way most kids learn. Did you know that she tried it once, too?

JOY: I guess I'm not surprised. A lot of people do try it. Did your mom spank you or punish you when she found out that you had tried it?

C. J.: No. She said that getting sick was punishment enough.

JOY: Well, do you think you'll smoke again?

C. J.: Heck no! It's terrible!

A final illustration of disciplining through natural consequences is in the incident that happened in my family when I was a child. Ron, my older brother who was in high school at the time, decided to go into business for himself. He smuggled some firecrackers in from Mexico and sold them to his friends and other kids in the neighborhood for quite a profit. Unfortunately, he sold some to a boy who set them off in a field of dry weeds. The weeds ignited and the fire department had to be called to put out the fire. An investigation traced the cause of the fire to Ron, who was then asked to report to the police station with the remainder of his firecrackers. I remember my parents being extremely upset about the whole thing. Most parents would have done anything to get their kid "off the hook," but wisely, my parents decided to let Ron suffer the consequences of his mistake. Going down to the police station was hard on Ron and probably harder on my parents. Ron was severely reprimanded, but even worse, he lost his firecrackers. His business went down the drain, but Ron had learned a lesson that proved to be far more valuable than the firecrackers he lost.

Sometimes it is not possible to let natural consequences discipline the child. Some natural consequences are not practical or are too dangerous. It would be insane to allow a child to suffer the natural consequences of playing out in the street! In situations like this, it's time to use what Rudolph Dreikurs calls LOGICAL CONSEQUENCES. Logical consequences are inflicted consequences that relate directly to the misbehavior. A logical consequence would be like making a child pay for something he has broken or not allowing a child who never eats at mealtime to snack between meals. Another example of a logical consequence is one that Dawn's mother set up for her.

DAWN: My mother doesn't want me to ride my Big Wheel out in the street.

JOY: If you did, what would she do to you?

DAWN: She wouldn't let me ride my Big Wheel for a whole week.

JOY: What do you think about that?

DAWN: I think it's fair.

Dawn was five years old. Aaron, an eleven-year-old girl, suffered a logical consequence of a different kind. Here's what she had to say about it.

AARON: Once, my teacher wrote a letter home to my mom. She said I wasn't doing my homework.

JOY: Oh? Was it true?

AARON: Yes.

JOY: Why weren't you doing your homework?

AARON: Because I was watching TV all the time.

JOY: What did your mom do?

AARON: She said I couldn't watch TV unless I got my homework done, and if she found that I didn't do it, she wouldn't let me watch any TV for a week.

JOY: Did you think that was fair?

AARON: Sure!

If your child continues to misbehave after you have conscientiously tried all four levels of discipline, then you will have to pull out your "ace in the hole," but only as a last resort. When all else fails, INFLICTED CONSEQUENCES are in order. Inflicted consequences include:

- Isolation (sending the child to his bedroom, making him sit in a chair, etc.)
- Deprivation (taking away something that is meaningful to the child, i.e., not allowing him to have dessert after dinner, taking away his bike for a week, "grounding" him, etc.)
- Corporal punishment (spankings)

Inflicted consequences are effective only when used sparingly. Like anything else, a child can become immune to isolation, deprivation, and corporal punishment. A social worker once told me, "The juvenile delinquents that we get are too tough to care any more. They have been punished so much that they have become immune to it. Nothing we are able to do gets to them." This is why I caution parents to try everything else first. Too often and too quickly parents jump to the fifth level of discipline without first trying the other four.

I had a parent once tell me that whenever her child did something wrong, the child would feel so guilty that she would go get the paddle and beg to be spanked. The mother would then proceed to spank her in order to relieve the child's guilty feeling. The mother told me that a psychologist condoned this procedure by telling her that "Children need to be released from guilt!" Feeling guilty to the extent that the child confesses to a wrong-doing and asks forgiveness is one thing, but when a child has been conditioned to feel guilty to the extent of begging for a spanking, something is not right.

I always tell parents who are concerned about relieving their child's guilt feelings that nothing works quite as well as an old-fashioned "I forgive you"! I agree that sometimes restitution is in order. For instance, if a child has broken something, he should have to help in replacing it, or if he has taken something that does not belong to him, he should return it. However, I refuse to believe that inflicted consequences are the only way to relieve a child's guilt feelings.

A good example of what I'm talking about is the time when Lisa decided to take some money out of the offering plate at Sunday school instead of putting her money in. All the way home I noticed her clutching something tightly in her fist and seeming to feel guilty about whatever it was. Finally, she burst into tears. Holding her open hand up to me, she revealed two quarters. "I took these from God," she said. "How do you feel about it?" I asked. "Very bad," she said. "I feel so sorry, but what shall I do now?" "The best thing to do is to return the money," I said. "But will God ever forgive me?" she questioned between sobs. I reminded her of the stories I had told her about God forgiving people. She returned the money, accepted God's forgiveness (and mine) and that was the end of it. Inflicted consequences were *not* needed to relieve her guilt.

Children have a lot of feelings about inflicted consequences. It comes up a lot in their discussions of parent–child relationships. Here is a collection of children's responses regarding inflicted consequences.

> KRISTY: When my mom spanks me, she uses a wooden spoon.
>
> JOY: How does it make you feel?
>
> KRISTY: Bad.
>
> JOY: Does it make you think about what you've done wrong?
>
> KRISTY: No. It makes me think about how mad I am at her. I want to hurt her back.
>
> JANET: My mom smacks me in the face when I get sassy.
>
> JOY: What do you do?
>
> JANET: I shut up. I don't sass her out loud, but I do in my mind.
>
> LORRIE: Spankings make me feel like a child.
>
> TRICIA: Spankings make me feel like a kid, too!
>
> JOY: Do you think you are a kid?
>
> TRICIA: I guess I am, but I'm not too little to work hard!
>
> MICHAEL: I don't mind getting spanked.
>
> JOY: Really? Why?
>
> MICHAEL: Because I think it makes my dad feel better.

Preventing Misbehavior

In contrast to the five levels of discipline that are designed for use after misbehavior occurs, there are three levels of discipline that can be used to prevent misbehavior. When it comes to misbehavior, it is good to remember that "an ounce of prevention is worth a pound of cure!"

The first level of misbehavior prevention is—you guessed it—MEETING THE CHILD'S NEEDS. We have discussed this before, so I'll move on to the next level.

COMMUNICATION is the second level of preventative discipline. Many times, telling a child how he should act and why is enough. Generally speaking, children enjoy pleasing others. They just need to be told how to go about doing it.

The third level involves MOTIVATING the child to "be good." This can be done in a variety of ways. The two methods that have been most successful for me as teacher and parent are the *contract* and the *chart* systems. Both of these systems have been in existence, in one form or another, for a very long time.

The contract system involves the preparation of a contract between the parent and child. The contract should be written simply enough so the child can understand it. It should also include the following four items:

1. What the child promises to do for the parent.
2. What the parent promises to do for the child.
3. What will happen to the child if he breaks his promise.
4. What will happen to the parent if he breaks his promise.

Here is a sample of a contract that was written for Leah, an eight-year-old girl, and her father.

1. Leah will promise to do the following things every day without being told:
   - Empty the waste paper baskets.
   - Make her bed.
   - Feed the cat and dog.

- Put her clothes in the dirty-clothes hamper.
- Pick up her personal belongings.

2. Daddy promises to pay Leah an allowance of 70¢ per week (10¢ per day) without being reminded.

3. Leah will give up 10¢ for each day that she does not do all she has agreed to do.

4. Daddy will pay Leah a double allowance in the event that he does not pay the allowance on time or if he has to be reminded. The allowance is to be paid on Saturday morning.

When using the contract system, it is necessary to follow certain rules. To begin with, both the parent and the child should be in on the setting up of the terms of the contract. Input from both sides should be considered until all terms are acceptable to each. One-sided contracts never seem to work.

The second rule would suggest that both the parent and the child be reasonable and realistic. No one should be required to do the impossible. Parents need to see that children do not agree to do more than they can realistically do. It is common for children to agree to "almost anything" at the time the contract is being written. When children agree to give more than they are capable of giving, they end up not meeting the terms of the contract and the whole bargain goes down the drain. Each time this happens, the child gets more and more suspicious of the contract system. Many children end up saying, "Contracts don't work." The same applies to the parents. They should never make promises on a contract that they cannot keep.

Rule number three is to make sure that everyone is satisfied with what they are getting out of the bargain. Every child has something that is worth working for. For some children, it is money; for some it is privileges; for others it could be something else.

A fourth rule to remember when using the contract is to *stick to it*. The contract should be set up for a certain period of time and should not be revised until that time has expired. Too often children get discouraged too soon and want to change the contract before it has had a chance to prove itself. It's hard to have faith in a contract that is constantly being revised.

The fifth rule is for parents only. Do not fulfill your part of the bargain until your child has done his part. In other words, do not advance the payoff. Also, giving him additional payoffs "on the side" is extremely counter-productive. If you're giving a child money all week long every time the ice cream truck passes or every time you go to the store, an allowance won't mean much. If the allowance proves to be insufficient, raise the allowance, don't supplement it.

	S	M	T	W	T	F	S	S	M	...
I brushed my teeth today without being told										
I picked up my clothes without being told										
I put all my toys away before bedtime										
I did what mommy or daddy said right away										
I was nice to Lisa all day										
I said my prayers before I went to sleep										
I went to bed without complaining										
I didn't yell for mommy to do things										
I got dressed by myself										

The last rule suggests that the contract be put in a place that is accessible to both parent and child so that it can be referred to as often as necessary.

Another good motivational tool is the chart. Charts are usually set up on a weekly or a monthly basis. They include a list of responsibilities that are to be completed by the child daily. Every day the list is reviewed by the parent and child and the child is rewarded a "star" or a "check" for each fulfilled responsibility. A specific number of stars or checks will earn the child a special reward at the end of the day, week or month, depending upon how immediate the rewards need to be. Younger children usually respond better to daily rewards, while older children sometimes enjoy working toward a larger payoff.

Here is an example of a chart that was set up for Christopher when he was four years old.

Like the contract, the following rules should be observed when making a chart:

1. The chart should be compiled by both the parent and child.

2. The items in the chart should be reasonable and realistic.

3. Everyone should be satisfied with what they are getting out of the bargain.

4. The chart should not be revised until it has had enough time to prove itself.

5. Parents should avoid premature or supplementary payoffs.

6. The chart should be kept in a place that is easily accessible to both the parent and the child.

A parent using the contract or the chart system should not have to punish the child. The child actually punishes himself by failing to keep his end of the bargain and thus subjects himself to the negative consequences which are built into the contract or the chart. This releases the parent from "riding herd" on a child and inevitably tends to enhance the parent-child relationship. It also forces the child to assume the responsibility for the punishment he receives.

A fourth level of preventative discipline is simply AFFIRMA-TION. The best way to perpetuate good behavior is to affirm it. When your child is being good, pay attention to him and bring to his attention the fact that you notice and appreciate his good behavior. Unfortunately, many parents notice children only when they misbehave.

We have discussed several ways of disciplining a child. A good disciplinarian will determine which form of discipline should be used in correcting a specific kind of misbehavior and then he will skillfully use it. Every parent has the potential of being a good disciplinarian and he can be one by being a parent who:

1. *Has a positive relationship with the child.* All of us have difficulty being disciplined by people we do not like because we become defensive and resist the discipline.

2. *Is able to forgive.* This includes forgetting! Nothing is worse than having to suffer continual chastisement and punishment for past acts of misbehavior. When a child misbehaves, the parent should discipline him and then forgive and forget.

3. *Is unselfish.* A disciplinarian who is unselfish will not limit discipline to misbehavior that is detrimental to himself. Too often we are motivated to discipline a child only when our rights have been infringed upon. It is good to remember that discipline should also be used to help a child avoid bringing harm to himself.

4. *Has reasonably pure motives.* The disciplinarian must want what is best for the child and the child needs to know that this is true.

Summary

The following chart will help to visualize the steps in the disciplinary process.

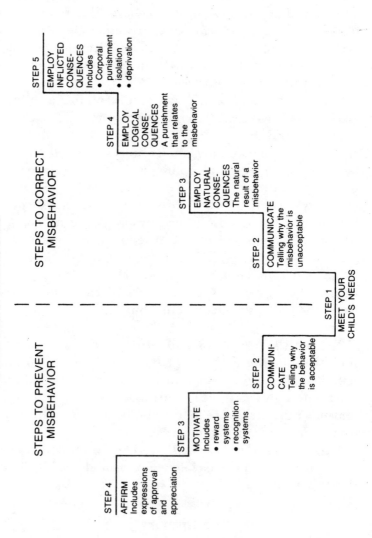

DISCIPLINARIAN PROCEDURES

STEPS TO PREVENT MISBEHAVIOR

STEP 4
AFFIRM
Includes expressions of approval and appreciation

STEP 3
MOTIVATE
Includes
• reward systems
• recognition systems

STEP 2
COMMUNICATE
Telling why the behavior is acceptable

STEP 1
MEET YOUR CHILD'S NEEDS

STEPS TO CORRECT MISBEHAVIOR

STEP 2
COMMUNICATE
Telling why the misbehavior is unacceptable

STEP 3
EMPLOY NATURAL CONSEQUENCES
The natural result of a misbehavior

STEP 4
EMPLOY LOGICAL CONSEQUENCES
A punishment that relates to the misbehavior

STEP 5
EMPLOY INFLICTED CONSEQUENCES
Includes
• Corporal punishment
• isolation
• deprivation

Other important points that were discussed in this chapter include:

A. Discipline is an educational process whereby a person learns what behavior is not acceptable and why it is not.

B. Punishment is an inflicted consequence which a person receives for misbehavior.

C. Misbehavior is that behavior which:
   1. hinders one's relationship with God.
   2. harms oneself or hinders one from realizing his potential and achieving his goals.
   3. infringes upon the rights of others.

D. Misbehavior is caused by:
   1. unfulfilled needs.
   2. a lack of understanding.
   3. thinking that misbehavior is more desirable than acceptable behavior.
   4. rebellion.

E. A contract should be simple and include four things:
   1. what the child promises to do for the parent.
   2. what the parent promises to do for the child.
   3. what will happen to the child if he breaks his promise.
   4. what will happen to the parent if he breaks his promise.

F. There are six rules for setting up a contract or a chart.
   1. The contract or chart should be compiled by both the parent and the child.
   2. The contract or chart should include reasonable and realistic demands.
   3. Everyone should be satisfied with what they are getting out of the bargain.
   4. The contract or chart should not be revised until it has been given enough time to prove itself.
   5. Parents should avoid "premature" and/or "supplementary" payoffs. Research shows that payoffs should be given as close to the desired behavior as possible.

6. The contract or chart should be kept in a place that is easily accessible to both the parent and the child.

G. A good disciplinarian:

1. has a positive relationship with the child.
2. is able to forgive and forget.
3. is unselfish.
4. has reasonably pure motives.

9

Rule #67—Don't Play Marbles for Keeps!

Values Clarification, Problem Solving, and Decision Making

I would like to begin this chapter with a discussion about the *Christian value system* and what Christians call the *world's value system* because of the influence that these two systems seem to have on the lives of children. Unfortunately, most children find themselves caught somewhere between the two systems, unable to decide which system to commit themselves to. It's like the confused little girl who once told me, "I honestly and truly want to do what's right—but not really!"

The Christian Value System

Recently a friend and I saw a movie about a compulsive gambler. Until that time I had no idea that gambling could become such a serious problem. After the movie was over, I remember remarking to my friend, "Now I know why I was never allowed to play marbles for keeps!"

The "don't-play-marbles-for-keeps" rule was typical of a whole list of rules that I never really understood or believed in, but was forced to follow as a child. The rules had been established for me by the people in the Christian community that I was a part of.

It was believed by them that if a person was really a Christian, he would naturally embrace the Christian value system and whether or not he actually embraced that system was made apparent by his willingness and ability to follow a specific list of rules. The list included such absolutes as no dancing, no drinking, no smoking, no going to movies, no card playing, etc. If a person did not follow all of these rules, it was thought by some that he was not really a Christian.

I later observed that the people who allowed their lives to be governed totally by the rules lost the sensitivity and flexibility that is so vital to living a Christian life. Generally speaking, they got so caught up in the "dont's" (don't do this and don't do that) that they didn't have time for the "do's" (do be loving, do be kind).

The Christian value system is based on a desire to love God, love yourself, and love others. The values that characterize the system are referred to as the "fruits of the Spirit." These two things never change, but *the way one goes about implementing the Christian value system will vary from person to person,* depending upon:

1. the time in which one lives.
2. the culture in which one lives.
3. the people that one is involved with.
4. the institution that one is a part of.

A person who adopts the Christian value system is not required to live a life that is identical to other Christians. Using the Bible and other valid sources, every Christian has the right to decide for himself how he will implement the Christian value system.

The World's Value System

According to the Christian faith there is a second value system called "the world's value system." It is based on the desire to love oneself above all else and sometimes at the expense of others. Christians refer to the values that characterize this system as "worldly values."

The chart on the next page, compiled by a group of junior-high and high school youth in a values clarification class, contrasts the two systems.

Teaching Values

A value is "something that is desirable or worthy of esteem for its own sake." When a person values something, it becomes worthy of that person's time, possessions, and efforts.

Values play an important part in one's life because they influence a person's behavior. What a person thinks, how he acts, and who he is are often a reflection of what he values.

I believe that values can be taught. They can be taught to a child by his parents and the people around him. Many values are taught overtly, others are taught in a subtle way.

Values that are subtly taught often become buried in a person's subconscious and, although the person claims that he does not think a certain way, his behavior indicates that he does. For example, some people claim that they are not racially prejudiced, but they purposely avoid having any contact with people of other races. I've seen it work the other way, too. I've known people who verbally say they value something, but their behavior says that they do not. This story is a good illustration of what I mean.

> We were sunning by an Olympic-sized swimming pool in the backyard of a gorgeous, eight-bedroom home. The housekeeper had just brought out an ice-cold pitcher of lemonade when the "lady of the house," an extremely wealthy widow, spoke up. "Joy, I invited you here today to talk about the new project for underprivileged children that you spoke of in the meeting the other night. I understand you need money to get the project

	THE CHRISTIAN VALUE SYSTEM	THE WORLD'S VALUE SYSTEM
The basis for the system	A desire to Love God Love Yourself Love Others	A desire to love yourself above all, often at the expense of others.
The values	"FRUITS OF THE SPIRIT" Love Joy Peace Forbearance Kindness Generosity Fidelity Gentleness Self-control	"WORLDLY VALUES" Money Material possessions Success Prestige Power Popularity/Fame Beauty Youth Fun and thrills
Behavior exemplifying the values	• Treat others as you would want them to treat you. • Don't confuse true happiness and joy with "having fun" • Avoid fights • Be patient with others; Don't demand too much from them too fast • Be willing to share your time, efforts and possessions with those who are needy • Stick by your friends even when they are down • Do not allow bad things to get control of your life • Be gentle and kind even if others think it's "sissy" • Do not do anything that would bring harm to yourself or others	• Be dishonest • Take things that are not rightfully yours • Compete • Put down anyone who gets in your way • Take advantage of weak people • Sacrifice anything (including morals) to become well known • Spend any amount of time, effort and money necessary to become beautiful and stay young • Risk anything to have fun

started?" "Yes," I said. She continued, "I've made it a policy to never give money to organizations that 'come begging.' A person could go broke if they gave to every philanthropic organization that asked for money! However, the most important thing to me is children, especially underprivileged children, and your project seems very worthwhile. In reality, it's the first project I've decided to contribute to in the last three years. I don't even give to the church anymore. They don't know how to manage money properly and I'm not giving them my money to throw away! But that's the point—your project deals with something that is really important to me and I want to help out. I've written a check. I want it to be used to get the project under way. Don't forget to get it from me before you leave today."

We sunned for a while longer, then played a set of tennis on the private tennis court behind the swimming pool area. We finished off the afternoon with a refreshing dip in the pool. As I was leaving, I was given a white envelope which contained the check.

I could hardly wait to get back to my office to open the envelope. In fact, I didn't wait. As soon as I was around the corner, I pulled my car over to the side of the road. Could this be the $2000 that is so desperately needed to make the program a reality? I thought as I tore into the envelope. I held the check in my hand and stared at it. "Fifty and 00/100 Dollars" had been neatly imprinted on it by a personalized check-writing machine.

I reflected back on what the lady had told me earlier in the afternoon: "The most important thing to me is children, especially underprivileged children." I couldn't help but think that the man-

ner in which she lived was a contradiction of what
she said.

Lots of parents are guilty of doing the same thing. They
say that they value specific things, but their behavior does
not support what they say. This is tough on children! The
old "Do as I say, not as I do!" statement that many parents
throw at their kids just doesn't work.

Kids end up saying, "If what they are telling me to do is
right, why don't they value it themselves?" It's like the little
five-year-old neighbor boy who came over to play with Lisa.
Lisa had two candy bars that I had instructed her to share
with her friend. One candy bar she liked; the other one she
didn't. She clutched tightly onto the one she liked and
offered the other one to the boy saying, "This is the best
one!" The boy reached for the candy bar that Lisa was
saving for herself. "If it's so good, why don't you want to
keep it for yourself?" he asked.

"Telling" your child something is not as effective as
"showing" him by the way you live. Edgar Guest wrote a
poem entitled, "Teacher's Example" that best illustrates
what I mean.

> I'd rather see a sermon
>   than hear one any day.
> I'd rather one should walk with me
>   than merely point the way.
> The eye's a better pupil
>   and more willing than the ear.
>
> Fine counsel is confusing
>   but, examples are always clear.
> And the best of all the preachers
>   are the men who live by their creeds.
> For to see good put into action
>   is what everybody needs.

I soon can learn to do it
   if you'll let me see it done.
I can see your hands in action,
   but your tongue too fast may run.
And the lectures you deliver
   may be very fine and true,
But I'd rather get my lesson
   by observing what you do.
For I may misunderstand you
   and the high advice you give,
But there's no misunderstanding
   how you act and how you live.*

Teaching and Applying
the Value System to One's Daily Life

Let's assume for a moment that we have successfully, through word and deed, taught our child about the value system that we want him to follow.

Your job is now only half over. At this point, the child must be taught how to apply the value system to his daily living. Many parents think that this means establishing a set of rules for the child.

To begin with, it is impossible to make up enough rules to cover every situation.

One day I watched a neighbor lady separate a boy and girl who had gotten into a fist fight. "Patrick! You know better than this!" she scolded. "What do you think your father would say about this?" Patrick answered, "He said, 'Don't get in fights with other boys,' but he didn't say anything about fighting with girls!"

In addition to this problem, there's a problem with making sure that a child obeys all the rules all the time. Trying to do this usually involves a great deal of punishment. More

---

* Reprinted from *Collected Verse* by Edgar A. Guest, copyright © 1934 by Reilly & Lee, a division of Henry Regnery Co., Chicago. Used by permission.

times than not, children obey rules, not because they accept them or think that they are fair, but because they fear being punished. In these situations, a child will disobey the rules whenever the threat of punishment is removed (when his parents aren't around).

This is why I believe in bringing children in on deciding how they are going to go about implementing their value system. When they are brought into making the rules they are going to live by, they will obey them because they choose to, not because they fear being punished.

Better than teaching a child what is right and what is wrong (setting up the rules for him) is teaching him how to determine for himself what is right and what is wrong (teaching him how to wisely set up his own rules).

In order to do this, we will need to teach our children how to solve problems and make decisions. They have the ability to do both of these things. It is a simple matter of giving them the tools.

Here are six steps which I recommend be followed when solving problems and making decisions.

	PROBLEM SOLVING	DECISION MAKING
Step 1	Define the problem	Define the decision to be made
Step 2	Determine the possible solutions	Determine the possible alternatives
Step 3	Choose the best solution	Choose the best alternative
Step 4	Solve the problem	Make the decision
Step 5	Accept the consequences	Accept the consequences
Step 6	Evaluate the whole process and determine if you would solve a similar problem the same way in the future.	Evaluate the whole process and determine if you would make a similar decision the same way in the future.

Here is a story that may help you to better understand this method of problem solving. It's about a fifth grade boy named Jon. Jon was an extremely intelligent Christian boy. He was small for his age and very non-aggressive. There was a bully at school that was continually hassling him. His first reaction was to get back at the bully by reporting him to the teacher. However, Jon took his Christianity seriously and he felt that he would rather not return evil for evil.

He came to see me one day after school. He shared the problem with me and we proceeded to go through the six steps of problem solving in the following manner.

Step 1—Define the problem. Jon had already defined the problem, so we moved on to step two.

Step 2—Determine the possible solutions. In Jon's words, the possible solutions as he saw them were

    a. tell on the bully and get him in trouble.

    b. take Karate lessons and get strong enough to "pound the bully into the ground."

    c. stay away from the bully.

    d. become friends with the bully.

Step 3—Choose the best solution. We went through the whole list. Solution "a" was eliminated because Jon didn't feel right about tattling on the bully. Solution "b" was eliminated because Karate lessons were too expensive and would take too long. Solution "c" was eliminated because Jon and the bully sat together in the same class and Jon couldn't avoid him. Solution "d" seemed like the best solution, so we talked about how it could be accomplished and Jon left.

Step 4—Solve the problem. The next day, Jon slipped a note to the bully during class. The note said, "I have fifty cents. If you will come with me to the Tastee Freez after school, I will buy you an ice cream cone." The bully was surprised, but accepted the offer. At the Tastee Freez, Jon talked to the bully. "I want to be your friend. Will you be my friend?" Under those circumstances, how could the bully refuse?

Step 5—Accept the consequences. Fortunately, there

weren't any negative consequences that Jon had to accept.

Step 6—Evaluate. Two weeks later, Jon came into my office with a big smile on his face. "How are things going?" I asked. "Fine! I got me a new friend!"

The decision-making process is similar to the problem-solving process. The following will illustrate this process.

Step 1—Defining the decision to be made. Lisa had been invited to a birthday party. On the same day of the party some friends of ours were going to be coming to our house and Lisa wanted very much to see them. She really didn't want to go to the party, but she was the only person invited and, being sensitive, she did not want to hurt the feelings of the girl who had invited her. What should she do?

Step 2—Determining the alternatives. Lisa thought of all the alternatives that were available and I listed them.

    a. We could have the birthday party at our house and even our visitors could come.

    b. We could have our visitors attend the birthday party at the other girl's house.

    c. Lisa could attend the party and see the visitors at another time.

    d. Lisa could pretend she was sick.

    e. I could call and tell the girl that Lisa couldn't come.

Step 3—Choosing the best alternative. Alternative "a" was ruled out because we were not really prepared to give a birthday party. Alternative "b" was unacceptable because the visitors did not know the girl giving the party and they would probably feel uncomfortable if they went to her party. Besides, they weren't invited! Alternative "d" was disallowed because it was not the truth. Alternative "e" was also omitted for the same reason. Alternative "c" was chosen—not with complete satisfaction on the part of Lisa, but with the realization that it was the best of the available alternatives.

Step 4—Making the decision. Lisa made the decision and went to the birthday party.

Step 5—Accepting the consequences. It was hard to accept the consequences of not seeing the visiting friends.

Step 6—Evaluation. When I picked Lisa up from the party, she was a bundle of excitement, telling me about all the fantastic things they got to do. All in all, she really enjoyed the party and it made her feel good that she had not hurt her friend's feelings by not going.

Not all decisions that children make have happy endings. Chris decided to get some high-top tennis shoes one time, saying that he would accept the consequences of having to struggle them on every morning. After the second day, he was begging for another pair of shoes. "No," I said. "When you decided to get those shoes, you were given the alternatives. There were at least two other alternatives that I *strongly* suggested, but my suggestions were ignored, and you chose the high-tops!" For six months he suffered the consequences of his decision. The next time we went in for shoes, he was not hesitant to solicit my advice on which alternative was best. I must add at this point that solving problems and making decisions are both processes that require a long time to develop. Begin by allowing your child to make small decisions and solve small problems. As he gets better at both processes, he can be given more responsibilities. One of the ultimate goals of parenting should be to get children to the place where they are solving most of their own problems and making most of their own decisions.

The great thing about teaching your child how to formulate his own rules is that the better he becomes at it, the less pressure there is on you to make the rules and follow up on them. Also, your child will be far more inclined to value, respect and abide by the rules he has formulated himself.

Summary

A. The Christian value system and what Christians call the "world's value system" seem to have a tremendous influence on the lives of children.

B. The Christian value system is:
  1. based on the desire to love God, love oneself, and love others.
  2. characterized by values that are referred to as the "fruits of the Spirit."
C. The Christian value system never changes, but the way in which one goes about implementing it will vary from person to person, depending upon the following four factors:
  1. the time in which one lives.
  2. the culture in which one lives.
  3. the people with whom one is involved.
  4. the institutions with which one is affiliated or involved.
D. The "world's value system" is
  1. based on the desire to love oneself above all else.
  2. characterized by values that are referred to as "worldly values."
E. Values can be taught. Sometimes they are taught overtly and sometimes they are taught subtly.
F. Children become confused when their parents say that they value Christian values, but live by worldly values.
G. The best way to teach a value system to a child is to "live it."
H. After a child has formulated his values, he then needs to be shown how to implement them into his daily living.
 I. Implementing one's value system involves knowing how to solve problems and make decisions.
 J. There are six steps to solving problems. They are:
  1. define the problem.
  2. determine the possible solutions.
  3. choose the best solution.
  4. solve the problem.
  5. accept the consequences.
  6. evaluate the process to determine its value for future use.

K. There are six steps to making decisions. They are:
   1. define the decision to be made.
   2. determine the possible alternatives.
   3. choose the best alternative.
   4. make the decision.
   5. accept the consequences.
   6. evaluate the process to determine its value for future use.
L. When children know how to solve problems and make decisions, they can formulate rules for behavior that will support their value system.

10

Grandma Just Died . . . But Don't Feel Bad!

Handling Feelings

I had been invited to observe a kindergarten class. The teacher had been in one of my "Rhythm and Body Movement" seminars and was anxious to show me how she had applied what she had learned. As I approached the room, I heard twenty-four voices belting out one of their favorite Hap Palmer songs.*

Sometimes I'm feeling happy and I'm wearing a smile;
Let me show you how I look when I'm feeling happy.

Sometimes I'm feeling sad and I'm wearing a frown;
Let me show you how I look when I'm feeling sad.

Well, feelings don't always stay the same—they can change;
Sometimes I'm happy, sometimes I'm sad. It's OK, it's not
    bad.

Sometimes I'm feeling angry and I stamp my feet;
Let me show you how I look when I'm feeling angry.

* "Feelings" from *Getting to Know Myself*, AR543 copyright © 1972 by Activity Records, Inc., Freeport, N.Y., 11520. All rights reserved.

"Things have sure changed!" I said to myself. "When I was a child, kids were told that anger and sadness came straight from the devil!"

I always had a hard time accepting that. I remember asking my seventh grade Sunday school teacher, "If God never makes mistakes and he created us with feelings, how could feelings be bad?" She couldn't give me an answer.

Another thing that had always stumped me was the fact that Jesus was perfect and yet he felt and expressed every kind of feeling imaginable, including anger, depression, grief, and sadness.

It wasn't until I became a teacher that the issue was resolved to my satisfaction. Deborah, a ten-year-old girl, made this statement during a classroom discussion on feelings: "It's not that feelings are bad, it's that sometimes they make you do bad things!"

That really made sense to me. Feelings, in and of themselves, are neither good nor bad. It's how one handles their feelings or what one does with them that becomes good or bad.

For a long time, it was highly inconceivable to me that anything good could come out of anger until I had the following experience.

One morning before class began, one of my boys came into the classroom, covered with bruises from head to toe. There was one spot on his head that looked particularly bad. When I asked him what had happened he said, "When my mother puts aspirin in her Coke, she turns crazy and does all kinds of crazy things." I rushed the boy to the office and reported the situation to my principal. The boy did not return to school for several days. When he returned, he acted as though nothing had happened and we never talked about the incident again.

About a month later, the boy came to school with bruises again covering his body, only this time he was in worse shape than he had been before. When I asked him what happened, he said that his dresser had fallen over on him.

I knew that this couldn't be true because there were bruises all over his legs and arms, as well as his head. I became so angry that I couldn't see straight! I took the boy to the office again, but this time I demanded to know what had been done the last time and what was going to be done this time. "Joy, stay out of this," my principal told me. "You can't prove anything really happened and if we say anything, we could all be sued for libel!"

I was so angry, I didn't care. In the days that followed, I found out that this boy had suffered many beatings before, some of which involved broken bones. But no one wanted to "get involved." My anger became so intense that I could not eat or sleep. I was driven to do something!

In the week that followed—and against the advice of several people to "not get involved"—I worked with the authorities to see that something was done to get the boy into a decent situation while his mother received help.

My anger had motivated me to get something done which needed to be done. This is the reason that people experience "negative" feelings. It is because these feelings often motivate people to get things done that need to be done. Like the person that is motivated to return to school because of his feelings of inferiority or inadequacy. Or the person who is motivated to become a part of a group because of his loneliness. Or the person who is motivated to give up the security of an old job for a new one because of the unhappiness he has experienced in his old job.

In these cases, feelings of inferiority, inadequacy, loneliness, and unhappiness contribute to positive ends.

I had a person tell me that once he became a Christian, God took away all of his negative feelings. He told me, "I never get angry any more. I'm never sad and I never get depressed!" He had been a Christian for two weeks.

Saying that God takes away all feelings of anger, sadness, and depression when one becomes a Christian is like saying that God takes away a person's arm or leg when he becomes a Christian. Feelings are a real and acceptable part of every person.

People who deny having certain feelings are only suppressing them. This is dangerous. When a person does not allow himself to express his feelings, or when other people will not allow him to express his feelings, they come out in subtle—many times, unacceptable—ways.

It's like a little girl I once knew who was never allowed to express her feelings of hatred and anger. She became an overly competitive person who turned every game she ever played into an opportunity to get angry and express hatred for her opponents. Things got so bad that no one ever wanted to play with her.

I knew of another child who was never allowed to express his feelings of resentment for his little brother. This boy had been an only child for six years. When the little brother came along, things changed. The older brother had horrible feelings of resentment toward his little brother, but his parents refused to deal with his resentment. They would constantly put the older brother down, saying that it wasn't right for him to beat up on his little brother.

One day in class, I held up a picture of a big boy beating up on a little boy. Here is what that big brother said about the picture: "He's hitting his little brother. He hates him. His mother likes the little brother. His mother does not like the big brother. His mother thinks that the little brother is perfect, but he's not as strong as me. I can beat him up. I'm better than he is! I really am!"

Parents should *not* encourage their children to squelch their negative feelings. Instead, they need to help them turn their negative feelings into positive behavior. It is only when a child is able to express his feelings that they can be dealt with.

There is a way to help your child effectively deal with his feelings. It involves four simple steps:

1. Identify the feeling.
2. Accept the feeling.
3. Determine what resulting behavior would be acceptable or not acceptable.
4. Encourage the child to express his feelings in an acceptable way.

I was a difficult child to handle. I can remember my mother telling me several times, "I hope you have a little girl just like you when you become a mother. Then you'll know what I've had to go through!" When Lisa was born, Mom's wish came true. I've been told by relatives that Lisa is "the spittin' image" of me. Like me, she is feisty and has quite a temper!

When she was about four years old, her anger was coming out in ways that were infringing on the rights of others. Whenever she became angry, she would pound on anything that was within reach—including me!

For several months we went through the four steps of dealing with feelings so many times that *she* had them memorized! At any rate, it worked! And here's how it did:

Step 1—Identify the feeling. Every time Lisa would get angry, I would say to her, "Lisa, you are angry."

Step 2—Accept the feeling. I would say to her, "I think I understand why you are angry. I get angry, too. Everyone gets angry at some time or another. It is not wrong for you to feel angry. Feeling angry is OK."

Step 3—Determine resulting behavior. "I understand that you need to get your angry feelings out, but hitting me and hitting other people is not a good way to get your anger out," I continued. "It's not fair to us. If you need to hit something, why don't you hit the couch or your bed or your pillow?"

Step 4—Encourage the child to express his feelings in an acceptable way. At that point, I would offer her an object which she would proceed to hit vigorously.

As time progressed, Lisa got to the place where, whenever she felt angry, she would run into her bedroom and beat on her pillow. After she had calmed down, we were able to deal in a positive way with the thing that had made her angry.

Sometimes, when a child expresses a negative feeling, it is a symptom of a deeper problem.

On a particular day, Patrick, one of the boys in the neighborhood, came over to play. The children were coloring on a large strip of butcher paper. One child accidentally scribbled on Patrick's part of the paper. Patrick flipped out! He ripped up the butcher paper, threw the crayons all over the room, and began beating up on anyone he could get his hands on.

His behavior was totally unacceptable, but somehow I couldn't help but feel that something else had contributed to that moment. Later on, during a conversation with his mother, I found out that Patrick was going into the hospital for a tonsillectomy. His mother said that he had been "on edge" ever since the day he had found out about the impending operation.

Feelings can serve as an indicator that a child may be undergoing serious problems. When a child overreacts to any situation, it is wise to find out why.

When thinking about feelings, negative or positive, we need to remember that maturity is not getting rid of certain feelings, but rather it is learning how to deal with them.

Summary

A. Feelings, in and of themselves, are neither good nor bad. It is how one handles feelings or what one does with them that becomes good or bad.

B. What is often referred to as "negative" feelings are sometimes necessary to motivate a person to do what needs to be done.

C. Feelings are a real and acceptable part of every person.

D. People who deny having certain feelings are only suppressing them.

E. When a person does not allow himself to express his feelings, or when other people will not allow him to express his feelings, they come out in subtle—often unacceptable—ways.

F. Parents should not encourage their children to squelch their feelings. Instead, they need to help them turn their negative feelings into positive behavior.

G. Parents can help their children deal with their feelings by following these four steps:

    1. Identify the feeling.

    2. Accept the feeling.

    3. Determine what resulting behavior would be acceptable or not acceptable.

    4. Encourage the child to express his feelings in an acceptable way.

H. Feelings can serve as an indicator that a child may be undergoing serious problems. When a child overreacts to *any* situation, it is good to find out why.

I. When thinking about feelings, we need to remember that maturity is not getting rid of certain feelings, but rather it's learning how to deal with them.

11

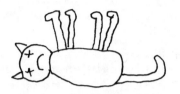

*Dealing with Death, Divorce
and Other Sticky Subjects*

Coping with Trauma—Part 1

"Christianity has nothing valid to say to children about
fear and trauma," a pediatric occupational therapist once
told me. I was just beginning as a director of children's min-
istries and, knowing that "hospital calls" would be a part of
my job description, I had sought the advice of an "old pro."
She continued to shock me by saying that "75-percent of my
time is spent undoing the damage that is done to children by
Christianity and the myths that Christians espouse and perpetuate." Defensively, I demanded that she be specific about
the myths that she was referring to. "There are a lot of them,"
she said, "but the ones that cause the greatest turmoil in the
children that I work with are:
- Christians *want* to die because when a Christian dies, he
  gets to go to heaven.
- Real Christians *never* experience fear because they know
  that God is with them.
- If a Christian doesn't get well, it's because he does not
  have enough faith that God will heal him.

- God *never* lets anything bad happen to Christians; he *always* keeps them safe.
- When something bad happens to a Christian, many times it is because he has done something wrong and God is punishing him for it.

"I suppose these myths were created to comfort and reassure people," the therapist continued, "but the guilt and confusion that they bring about is devastating."

I left the hospital thinking all kinds of terrible things about that therapist. "It's obvious," I said to myself, "that the lady just doesn't know what she is talking about!"

It wasn't until months later, while visiting a twelve-year-old terminal cancer patient at the City of Hope, that I began to understand what the therapist was talking about. "Why is God doing this to me?" Carl asked with tears in his eyes. "What could I have done to make him so mad?"

When my visit with Carl was over, his mother walked with me to my car. "I can't understand it," she said. "Carl is such a good boy and you know that our whole family has been a Christian family for years. Why would God let this happen to us?" "What about your husband?" I asked. "How does he feel about all of this?" "He refuses to accept the fact that Carl is dying," she told me. "He's certain beyond a shadow of a doubt that God is going to heal Carl."

When Carl finally died, his family and the small Christian community of which they were a part were confused and bewildered. I was concerned.

On the Friday following the funeral, I gathered together a small group of children that had known Carl. I was interested to find out how they perceived his death and if and how it had affected them. One boy grimly began the session. "If God did that to Carl, he might do that to me, too, huh?"

"So what?" replied one of the older girls. "If it happens to us, we'll get to go to heaven and my Sunday school teacher told me that going to heaven is funner than going to Disneyland!"

A third child responded, "Well, even going to Disneyland was scary the first time!"

The dialogue that continued convinced me that the myths I had heard about were, in fact, realities to these children.

Realizing that something had to be done, I set up my first "Sticky Subjects" class. The class was designed to "teach children how to cope with trauma." It was a tremendous success and, as a result, I have been stressing the need for this kind of education ever since.

Recently I was talking to a group of parents about trauma education when I was asked, "Where do we begin?" I answered by saying, "For those who believe in God, being able to cope with trauma begins with a belief in the following concepts:

1. God is perfect; he never makes mistakes.
2. God is in control.
3. God loves man.

"Once a child believes that these concepts are true," I continued, "he is better able to evaluate, understand, and accept trauma as he experiences it." "Well," another parent asked, "what do you say to a child who asks, 'If these things are true about God, why does he let bad things happen to me?'" I responded by saying, "I tell children that when they experience bad things, it is usually for one of two reasons. The first reason is: When a person makes a mistake—by breaking one of God's spiritual or physical laws—God allows that person to suffer the consequences of that mistake so that he will learn why he should avoid making that mistake again. ["Suffering the consequences" is often a traumatic experience.] The second reason is: Sometimes a person experiences a trauma through no fault of his own. God also allows this to happen so that the person can learn valuable lessons and continue to grow. For people who do not believe in God, it is still valid to stress the value and importance of viewing trauma as an educational experience."

How do children respond to this kind of teaching?

John had been in my "Sticky Subjects" class for seven weeks when his accident happened. In a hurry to get to school, he rode his bike through a red light and was hit by a car. I visited him in the hospital. "I guess I'll have to take the blame for this one," he told me. "For sure, it's not God's fault!" In the weeks that followed, I watched John suffer the consequences of his mistake without bitterness and without hostility. When the ordeal was over, he shared with the class, "This whole thing hasn't been much fun, but I sure learned a lot!"

On the evening of our last class, Kimberly (a sixth grader) was told that her parents were getting a divorce. Despairingly, she shared the news with me after church on Sunday morning. "Kim," I said, "your parents' divorce is not your fault. It is not your mistake." "I know!" she responded, "but I still feel terrible!"

During the next few months, Kim and I spent a lot of time together. Needless to say, her experience in the "Sticky Subjects" class made my job of counseling her a lot easier. Slowly, we worked our way through "The Six Steps of Coping with Trauma" that she had learned about in class.

Kimberly's parents were extremely appreciative of my efforts. Months later, her mother shared with me, "Kim is getting along just fine, thanks to her involvement with you and her experience in your 'Sticky Subjects' class. I only wish every child could have a similar opportunity."

Unfortunately, not all parents agree with Kimberly's mother. "I am very much opposed to teaching children about traumatic things!" one lady told me. "These children are too young to be exposed to the bad side of life. There's time enough for them to learn about these things when they get older!"

Two weeks later, a truck backed over her six-year-old nephew and killed him instantly. It grieved me to hear that the accident had happened and that the only witness present was her ten-year-old son.

Most of the time very little warning is given before a traumatic experience occurs. This is why I believe so strongly in "pre-trauma education." I've pre-educated my own children regarding certain traumas, and it has really paid off.

When Christopher was about four years old I took him on a field trip to the hospital. We visited the emergency room (at a time when it was not in use), and the nurse took us through the facilities, showing us the equipment and instruments. We made the outing a special one by eating lunch in the hospital cafeteria and buying a small toy from the hospital's gift shop. On the way home, I said to Christopher, "One day you may get very sick or badly hurt. If I am not able to fix you up with Band-aids I'll take you to the emergency hospital where they will be better able to fix you up."

Several months later Christopher was attacked by a large dog and was bitten badly on the forehead. He needed medical attention, so we took him to the hospital. On the way there, he looked up at me from my lap and asked, "Mommy, are you taking me to the place where they are going to fix me up?"

The doctors and nurses in the emergency room said that Christopher had been one of the best behaved emergency patients they had ever had. I attributed it to the fact that he had been pre-educated and therefore knew what to expect. This made him less fearful and more cooperative in the emergency room.

If you know that a trauma is going to happen (moving, hospitalization, etc.) pre-education will make the entire experience easier on everyone.

Getting a haircut is a mild trauma which most very young children have to go through at one time or another. Realizing this, I began to prepare Christopher for it ahead of time. Again, we took a field trip to the barber shop where everything was explained to him. A second trip was taken, but this time Christopher watched while I had my hair cut. Before going to the barber for the third time, I allowed Christopher to cut off—under my supervision—a lock of his hair. By doing this, he learned that getting his hair cut was not painful as many young children believe it to be. When Chris finally went in for his haircut, it was an enjoyable experience for everyone involved.

If you have not had an opportunity to pre-educate your child before he experiences a trauma, all is not lost. One way in which parents can help their child to handle a traumatic situation is by following these six steps:

1. Help the child to identify the trauma and its cause (s) .

2. Encourage the child to accept the trauma as a reality.

3. Assist the child in defining what his involvement was in causing the trauma.

4. Help the child to decide what he can do to alleviate the trauma.

5. Encourage the child to openly and honestly respond. Encourage him to share his feelings and assure him that his responses and feelings are understandable and acceptable.

6. Allow the child to continue to communicate with you about the trauma until the situation is resolved to his satisfaction—until he chooses to not talk about it further.

Earlier in this chapter, I made reference to helping Kim, the sixth-grade girl whose parents were getting a divorce, work her way through these six steps. So that you can better understand the practical application of the six steps, I am going to explain how they were applied to her situation.

Step 1: The situation and its causes had already been identified. Kim's parents told her that they were getting a divorce because they could not get along with each other.

Step 2: At that point, I encouraged Kim to accept the divorce as a reality.

Step 3: Our third step was to define what role Kim had played in causing the trauma. When it was determined that she had done nothing to cause the divorce—a factor which will not always be true for every trauma that a child experiences—we moved on to the next step.

Step 4: This was to decide what Kimberly was going to do about the whole situation. She finally concluded that there was nothing that she could do to stop the divorce from happening (both parents had told her that this was true) and that she would just have to accept it.

Step 5: Kim was encouraged to openly and honestly express her feelings about the divorce. I assured her that her feelings were understandable and acceptable and that she was quite "normal" for feeling the way she did.

Step 6: This step went on for quite a long time. Kimberly was allowed to talk about the divorce as often as she felt a need to do so, and I encouraged her to talk through the six steps until the issue was resolved in her mind.

"Talking through" the six steps for a child who has just experienced a death would go something like this:

Step 1: "As you know, John, Grandfather was very old. He had lived many years and had lived a very good life. The time has now come for him to die."

Step 2: "Everyone must die sometime. Grandfather died this morning and there is nothing anyone can do to change that fact."

Step 3: "It was not your fault that Grandfather died. There is nothing you did to make him die and there is nothing you could have done to keep him alive. You had nothing to do with Grandfather's death."

Step 4: "There is nothing you can do to bring Grandfather back to life again. You will never see him again while you are alive, but you can think about him as much as you want to and you can remember how much he loved you and how much you loved him. You can remember the fun times you had together and all the wonderful things he taught you. You will never see Grandfather again as long as you live, but you don't have to forget him."

Step 5: "How do you feel about all of this? How do you

feel about Grandfather dying?" Different children will give different answers. Some will feel grief, some will feel anger, others will feel guilt and so on. "John, I think I understand how you feel. Other people have probably felt the same way as you are feeling. It is normal for you to have feelings about Grandfather's death."

Step 6: "John, talking about Grandfather's death right now may not be enough. You may have other questions about it that you want to ask, or you may have other feelings which you want to tell me about. You might want to have me remember with you about the things you learned from Grandfather. Whenever you want to talk about Grandfather, I want to listen, so please come and share with me anything you need or want to talk to me about regarding him or his death."

To interpret the Christian view of death and dying to your child, it would help to add something like this.

In Steps 2 and 3, say, "God is in control of everything. He never makes mistakes. When he allowed Grandfather to die, it was for the best. We may not understand *how* it could be for the best because we can not understand how God thinks, but we must trust God that what he decides to allow is for the best."

In Step 4, say, "When Grandfather died, his spirit left to go and be with God. When you die, your spirit will also go to be with God, and then your spirit will be with Grandfather's spirit."

Whatever you do, be real and be honest. Sincerity is the key to helping anyone cope with trauma.

Summary

A. Religion has a tendency to perpetuate several myths. They are:

1. Christians *want* to die, because when a Christian dies, he gets to go to heaven.
2. Real Christians *never* experience fear because they know God is with them.
3. If a Christian doesn't get well, it's because he does not have enough faith that God will heal him.
4. God *never* lets anything bad happen to Christians; he *always* keeps them safe.
5. When something bad happens to a Christian, many times it is because he has done something wrong and God is punishing him.

B. Trauma education is designed to dispel these myths and help children to cope realistically with trauma.

C. For Christian parents, being able to cope with trauma begins with a belief in the following concepts:
    1. God is perfect.
    2. God is in control.
    3. God loves man.

D. Trauma should be viewed as an "educational experience."
    1. Pre-trauma education makes going through trauma easier on everyone.
    2. One way in which parents can help their children handle trauma is by following the "Six Steps for Coping with Trauma." They are:
        a. Help the child identify the trauma and its causes (s).
        b. Encourage the child to accept the trauma as a reality.
        c. Assist the child in defining what his involvement was in causing the trauma.
        d. Help the child to decide what he can do to alleviate the trauma.
        e. Encourage the child to openly and honestly respond. Encourage him to share his feelings and assure

him that his responses and feelings are understandable and acceptable.

  f. Allow the child to continue to communicate with you about the trauma until the situation is resolved to his satisfaction.

12

The Ten Plagues

Coping with Trauma—Part 2

Theresa's foster mother had brought her to see me. She was living in a foster home because her father had died tragically in an accident and her mother had married another man—who had molested Theresa and beaten her on several occasions. On the way to school one day, Theresa was hit by an automobile and ended up in the hospital for months with a broken back. All of this had put Theresa drastically behind in school and she had just been told that she would not be able to move up to the next grade with her class.

The foster mother brought Theresa to me to work out some tutoring arrangements. We talked for a while and then they left. As Theresa was leaving the office an older woman was coming in. When Theresa was out of sight, the older woman fondly remarked, "Ah, to be a child again! No worries, no problems! Life for a child is so simple, so uncomplicated!"

It never fails. At least once a week, some uninformed adult will make a similar remark—to which I reply, "You ought to know what I know!"

I know what I know because of the classes I've had with children in which traumas are discussed. Life isn't totally problem-free for anyone—including children.

Most of what I've learned about children and trauma is what I've learned by listening to kids talk. It doesn't take long to come to the conclusion that there are about ten traumas that seem to plague children the most. One of the boys in a "Sticky Subjects" class jokingly referred to these traumas as "The Ten Plagues." They are the following.

1. Separation—being separated from parents for short or long periods of time.
2. Nightmares.
3. Moving—to a different neighborhood, school, or church.
4. Adding a new person to the family—either a new baby or another adult (grandparent).
5. Visits to the doctor, dentist, and hospital.
6. Death.
7. Divorce.
8. Injuries and/or handicaps—either observing them or incurring them.
9. Adoption.
10. Sexual offenses.

Each of these traumas can be dealt with effectively by using the "Six Steps for Coping with Trauma" discussed in the preceding chapter, and by making note of certain guidelines that will be discussed in this chapter.

Separation

It was my first day as a preschool teacher and George's first day as a student. I was nervous and George was apprehensive. The only one who seemed to be on top of the situation was George's mother. Without batting an eyelash, she pushed George, kicking and screaming at the top of his lungs, into my arms. "He'll be all right in a few minutes," she said nonchalantly. "I've been through this with four others and they all survived. He'll get over it, too!" With that, she turned around and left.

How wrong she was! George didn't "get over it" for the rest of the day and for several days to come. George's mom assumed that he should have automatically known something that took his older brothers and sisters years to learn—that when their mother left, she would eventually return. This is not something a child automatically knows when he is born. It is something that every child must learn, and until it is learned, separation—no matter how long or how short—is painful.

Try to observe the following "Do's" and "Don'ts" when handling a separation situation. These have worked for me and other parents I know. I share them—not in a dogmatic way—but in hopes that you will use them as guidelines for handling your own situation in a creative and loving way.

STRIVE TO

A. Understand that, until a child learns differently, he undergoes feelings of abandonment when you leave him.
B. Remember that infants and young children do not have a sense of time. Therefore, saying that you'll "just be gone for a little while" is meaningless.
C. Begin by leaving your child for short periods of time with people he knows who will help him learn that you'll be back.
D. Follow this procedure when leaving your child:
  1. Give the necessary information, and anything else that may be necessary, to the adult that will be caring for the child.
  2. Gather everything you will be taking with you.
  3. Take a moment to explain to the child
     a. where you'll be going,
     b. what you'll be doing,

    c. when you'll be back,

    d. why the child can't come with you.

4. Make sure the child is securely with the adult that is caring for him—so he will not run after you.

5. Give the child a good-bye kiss and hug.

6. Leave immediately.

E. Have a few "practice runs" before leaving your child in a strange place. For example, if he is going to a new church or school, go and stay with him the first few times so that he has a chance to get used to the situation while you are there.

F. Allow him to take "security objects" (blankets, toys, etc.) with him from home if he is going to a strange place.

STRIVE NOT TO

A. It would be best not to return to the house or room after you have left.

B. It would be best not to linger after you have said good-bye.

C. It would be best not to collaborate with the adult who is caring for the child to distract him while you "sneak away." This will cause him to "cling" to you any time he fears that you may be leaving him.

If you feel that you have done everything possible to ease the pain of separation for the child, don't be intimidated by his tears or tantrums, and don't feel guilty.

Nightmares

Coping with trauma during the daytime is hard enough, but at 2:00 A.M. it's even worse. There's nothing more disconcerting than waking up from a deep sleep in response to a soft tap on the shoulder accompanied by the familiar sound of, "Mommy, I'm having bad dreams!" At that stage of the game, you couldn't care less whether or not there are a million snakes crawling all over the floor or a huge monster lurking in the closet. But nightmares *are* traumatic and need to be dealt with.

Strive To

A. Be empathetic and understanding.
B. Find out what the nightmare is about so that you can "talk it through" with the child.
C. Return to the child's bedroom with him.
D. Take a tour of the bedroom (or the entire house, if necessary) with the child, showing him that all is safe.
E. Tuck the child back into bed.
F. Stay in the room with him until he is not afraid to stay alone or until he goes back to sleep.
G. Reassure him that you will be in your bedroom and that he can call you or come and get you if he needs you again.
H. Sleep with the child or allow him to sleep with you *if* the nightmares persist on through the night.

Strive Not To

A. Do not trivialize the nightmare by saying things like "That's silly! There are no snakes on the floor!" or "Don't be foolish! There's no such thing as monsters!"
B. It would be best not to send the child back to his room alone.
C. It would be best not to leave the child before he feels good about your leaving.
D. It would be best not to make the child stay in his room by himself if he is still frightened.
E. It would be best not to take the child to bed with you immediately, before trying to resolve the nightmare for him. For everyone's sake, having the child come to bed with you should be the *last* resort.
F. It would be best not to allow your child to watch movies or experience things that will cause him to have nightmares.

Sometimes your child may go through a stage where he is having nightmares every night. When this occurs, he may be frightened to go to bed. If his fear is genuine, try this routine:

First night. Sit on his bed until he falls asleep.

Second night. Stay in the room until he falls asleep. Sit somewhere further away from the bed.

Third night. Sit in the doorway where he can see you until he falls asleep.

Fourth night. Stay just outside his door (where he cannot see you) until he falls asleep.

Fifth night. Assure him that you will be in the house and that you can come to him if he should need you. Promise to check in on him before you go to bed.

Moving

Recently my family and I changed churches. On the morning that we were to start attending the new church, I contracted a severe headache. The family decided to go on without me. Strangely enough, the minute they were out of sight, my headache went away! The next Sunday while we were getting ready for church, I developed an unbelievable stomach-ache. I was sitting on the edge of the bed, debating whether or not I should go, when Lisa came into the room and sat down beside me. Softly she patted me on the back and said, "Your problem is that you don't want to go to a new church! Don't be scared—we'll all be there with you!"

Lisa was right! I was experiencing the trauma of moving. There are a lot of feelings a person has to struggle through when he has to move. There is the feeling of sadness and grief when one leaves old friends, there is the fear of being rejected by the new people you will be meeting, there's the anxiety one experiences when he steps out into the "unknown." All in all, moving is a difficult process, but you can help your child come through it with flying colors.

STRIVE TO

A. Prepare the child ahead of time. As early as possible explain to him
   1. where he will be moving,
   2. what he will be doing there,
   3. exactly when he'll be moving,
   4. why he has to move.
B. Familiarize him with the place to which he will be moving. If possible, visit the new place several times before the move. When this is not possible, use pictures, maps, or anything else to acquaint him with the new place.
C. Accentuate the positive! There's a "good side" to almost everything a person does. Find out what the "good side" is and capitalize on it.
D. Involve the child in the actual moving process. Let him pack and unpack his own things if you are moving to a new home.
E. Encourage him to get the addresses and telephone numbers of his friends he will be leaving behind so that he can keep in touch with them.

STRIVE NOT TO

A. It would be best not to make false promises of "coming back" if they can't be kept.
B. It would be best not to force your child to make moves too often, unless they are absolutely necessary.

Adding a New Person to the Family

Sean shuffled into the classroom with his head bowed. "Sean, why so glum?" his teacher asked. "I heard that your mother just had a little baby boy! Just think—you've got a new brother!" "That's the problem!" Sean mumbled. "He's already started taking over all my things!" "Like what?" the teacher asked. "Like my bedroom!" Sean retorted.

Adding another person to the family is tough on children. Whether it's a baby or a grandparent, one more person means having to "give up" and "give in" a little more.

Here are some things to remember if this should happen in your family.

STRIVE TO

A. Warn the child before the new person arrives. This should be done as far in advance as possible.
B. Bring him in on the planning and preparation for the new person's arrival.
C. Let him know that, although he will be expected to share certain things (his bedroom, perhaps), there will be many things that he will not have to share unless he wants to.
D. Assure him of the fact that the new person's arrival will not make any difference in your relationship with him. He will still be important to you and he will still be loved by you just as much as ever.
E. Spend some quality time with the child on the day that the new person arrives.
F. Continue to be sensitive to the child, making sure that he is never "pushed aside" or "left out."

STRIVE NOT TO

A. It would be best not to make him feel guilty for any negative feelings he may have toward the new person. Help him to deal with them properly.
B. It would be best not to force him to give up too much for the new person.
C. It would be best not to expect too much out of him just because the new person has arrived. Don't force him to "grow up" overnight.
D. It would be best not to overload him with too much responsibility for the care of the new person too quickly.

Visits to the Doctor, Dentist, and Hospital

When I was a child I was hospitalized twice for major abdominal surgery. I thank God for having gone through these two experiences, because they prepared me for the four major surgeries I was to have later on in life (two of which involved cancer) .

Thanks to my mother sitting by the hour and sewing doll clothes for my "hospital doll" and doing things like painting my nails with fingernail polish while I was forced to stay in bed, my trips to the hospital weren't so bad.

When I got older and had to face hospitalization again, I wasn't afraid. The roommate I had during my last visit to the hospital wasn't as fortunate as I was. She had been told by her doctor that she had waited too long to have her surgery. By the time she came to the hospital, her condition had gotten out of control and there was nothing that could be done for her. "I always said that I'd rather die than go to the hospital," she told me on the afternoon I was leaving.

Several months later I found out that she did die. The nurse that told me about her death said that if she would have come to the hospital sooner, she could have been saved. "How sad!" I thought to myself. "It wasn't her illness that killed her as much as it was her fear!"

Visits to the doctor, dentist, and hospital can be positive experiences.

STRIVE TO

A. Precede emergency or sick calls with a field trip or a routine non-threatening check-up where nothing painful happens.

B. Tell the child about the visit ahead of time. Answer all of his questions as honestly as you possibly can.

C. Make preparations for the visit. If you are going to the doctor or dentist, it's good to bring something for the child to do while he is waiting so that he will not have a chance to conjure up any negative thoughts. If you are going to the hospital, it's always fun to purchase several inexpensive toys and wrap them up. Let the child open them, one at a time, whenever he gets bored.

D. Keep the child's mind occupied while he is waiting for the doctor, dentist, or operation.

E. Stay with the child for as long as you possibly can. Do not leave until he, the doctor, dentist or nurse, asks you to leave. I strongly recommend that parents spend the night with the child at the hospital, if at all possible.

F. Visit the local ice cream parlor or toy store after visiting the doctor or dentist. Make this a habit, so that your child will associate going to the doctor or dentist with pleasure instead of pain.

In regard to hospitalization, this is not the time to let your fears of "spoiling" your child take control. Shower him with love, attention and, if possible, gifts.

Strive Not To

A. It would be best not to let the child automatically assume that every visit to the doctor, dentist, or the hospital is a negative experience.

B. It would be best not to use frightening phrases like, "It's going to hurt," or "It's going to be painful." Instead, use phrases like, "You may be uncomfortable for a while," or "You may not like it."

C. It would be best not to go into any "gory details." Honesty is important, but not to the point of saying things like, "They will be cutting into you with a knife." Remember that a large percentage of fear is in one's mind.

D. It would be best not to insist that your child refrain from crying—especially if it means that you must resort to demoralizing phrases like, "Big boys and girls don't cry," "Brave people don't cry!"

Death

Believe it or not, children think a lot about dying. In a discussion with a group of first graders, these comments were made:

> LORI: I feel terrible about dying because I won't ever see my friends again.

> KENT: I don't want them to put me in the ground because then I couldn't breathe!

> LOUIS: They put you in the ground so that you can feed the flowers that they plant on top of you.

> ASHLUND: My grandma was cold when I felt her. Why didn't she put her sweater on?

> CARLA: It hurts to die. It hurts worse than a bad, deep cut.

> JOY: What makes you think that?

> CARLA: Because no one wants to die, just like no one wants to get cut!

Most children come into contact with death sometime during their childhood. Some lose relatives, others have pets that die. Death is thought by some to be the worst of all the traumas. I suppose that this is debatable but, nonetheless, coming into contact with death has the potential of affecting one negatively. Here are a few guidelines for helping your child cope with death.

STRIVE TO

A. Teach children about the cycle of life—the fact that, although everything has a beginning and an end, the end of one thing usually marks the beginning of something else.

B. Emphasize the fact that it is the quality of one's life which counts, rather than the "quantity."

C. Encourage the child to accept the fact that the deceased

has died. Then tell the child that, although he may never see the deceased on earth again, he can think about him and remember him.

D. Allow him to openly and honestly express his feelings about death.

STRIVE NOT TO

A. It would be best not to avoid talking about death if your child wants to talk about it, or if he has questions about it.

B. It would be best not to emphasize the morbid details about death.

C. It would be best not to "talk up" heaven too much. Too often, children feel guilty or feel that something is wrong with them if they don't want to die and go to heaven.

D. It would be best not to compare death with sleep. The child will be afraid to go to sleep.

E. It would be best not to say that the deceased died because he was "sick." The child will fear getting sick.

F. It would be best not to tell the child that the deceased has gone on a long trip.

G. It would be best not to give the child false hopes of the deceased returning.

H. It would be best not to allow the child to feel responsibility or guilt for the death of the deceased.

I. It would be best not to force a child to attend a funeral. Funerals are for adults, but let the child choose whether or not he wants to go.

Divorce

No matter how "civil" two people are to each other, divorce is not a pleasant experience. This is especially true when children are involved. For this reason, some adults choose to "stick it out," often "for the sake of the children." There can be some real disadvantages to doing this. I've known some parents to stay in a bum marriage for the sake of the children and then subtly resent the children for it. Parents somehow think that children are not smart enough to know what's going on. Again, here are some comments from children in the first through the third grades who have come from distressed homes:

> ANN: My parents really like each other. They just don't get along. Is that true?
>
> JOY: Why do you ask that?
>
> ANN: Because I don't like the people I don't get along with.
>
> HEIDI: My parents fight a lot.
>
> DAVID: Mine do, too! What do your parents fight about?
>
> THE GROUP: Money, my dad isn't home enough, my mom doesn't clean up the house.
>
> DAVID: It's the happiest around my house when mom or dad *isn't* home.
>
> JOY: Why?
>
> DAVID: Because it's quiet!
>
> HEIDI: *I* try my best, but my parents still argue.
>
> JONAS: When my mom and dad fight all the time, even our cat feels icky!

When all is said and done, most children will agree that parents do not do anyone a favor by perpetuating a bad relationship. Worse than going through a divorce is living in the fear that a divorce might happen. Children are like adults in that they find it easier to cope with realities than with unknowns.

We need to realize that:

● Two "bad" parents are not better than one "good" parent.
● Life can be successful and happy in homes where there is only one parent.
● Children can adjust to a divorce.

Here are some tips on how to help your child survive your divorce.

STRIVE TO

A. Be the first one to tell him about the divorce before someone from outside the home does.

B. Remember that there are *two* sides to every story. If the child hears any side at all, make sure that he has the privilege of hearing both sides.

C. Encourage the child to continue his relationship with the other parent. The child should not have to give up a relationship with one of his parents just because the parents decide to give up each other.

D. Encourage him to maintain relationships with relatives from "the other side."

E. Avoid fights over visitation rights, but if they should occur and if the child is within ear-shot, say something like, "Everyone loves you so much that they would like to have you all to themselves, but it looks like we're going to have to share you!"

F. If you have custody of the child, make sure that the other parent is adequately informed at all times as to what is happening in the child's life.

STRIVE NOT TO

A. It would be best not to ever blame the child for the divorce, and don't allow him to accept any responsibility for it. The inability of two adults to resolve their differences, solve their problems, or handle life's traumas should not be blamed on a child.

B. It would be best not to allow the child to feel that he was rejected (by the parent who left) because of his (the child's) inadequacies or inferiorities.

C. It would be best not to ever make a child choose which parent he likes best. If at all possible, do not make him decide which parent he prefers to live with. If the court should ask the child to choose which parent he would want to live with, I would recommend the following as being the best procedure:

1. Consult an unbiased child psychologist or family counselor for whom the mother, father, and child have a mutual respect.

2. After allowing him to study the situation carefully, have him (the counselor) make the decision for the child. A good psychologist or counselor will always take into consideration the wishes of the child.

3. In three to six months, with the assistance of the psychologist or counselor that made the initial choice, evaluate the situation and decide whether or not to continue with the original decision. The decision to keep or throw out the original choice should be based entirely upon what is best for the child.

D. It would be best not to involve the child in your arguments. Avoid the old "You tell your father . . ." or "You tell your mother . . ." routine.

E. It would be best not to use your child as a "spy" to keep you informed as to what the other parent is doing.

F. It would be best not to ever "put down" the other parent in front of the child.

G. It would be best not to allow the child to heap guilt upon you. Let him know that you made a mistake and that you are sorry, but life must go on.

H. It would be best not to allow the child to "play you against" the other parent. This is where a good relationship with the ex-spouse really pays off!

I. It would be best not to pressure the child to report every detail of his visit with the other parent. Let him tell you about it in his own way and in his own time.

J. It would be best not to allow the child to have false hopes that mom and dad will get back together if, in reality, they won't.

Injuries and/or Handicaps

One day I received a call from my son's school. I could hear Christopher crying hysterically in the background. The school principal asked if I could come to the school and talk to Chris. I hung up the phone and rushed to the school. When I arrived, I found Christopher slumped over in a chair in the office, with his face buried in his hands. I picked him up and took him outside. "Mommy, I want to leave this school and never come back again!" he sobbed. I couldn't understand it! He had been crazy about the school. I couldn't help but wonder what had caused the sudden change in attitude.

It took a long time, but he finally told me the reason. "Mike touched me!" he said, cringing. "So?" I responded. "I'm sure a lot of people have touched you today!" "But Mike's finger is horrible-looking," Chris went on. "He has a disease! Now I'm going to get it and all of my fingers are going to fall off!"

I later discovered that Mike had lost the tip of his index finger in a bicycle-wheel accident. Everything began to make sense now. For weeks, Chris had been having terrible nightmares about being chased by an ugly man with "long, skinny fingers." And now I could see why.

Mike's finger was Christopher's first encounter with a "handicap" and his reaction was completely normal. As we worked through this incident together, I took into consideration the following Do's and Don't's.

STRIVE TO TEACH YOUR CHILD THAT:

A. Handicaps can range from a deformed fingernail to total mental or physical disablement.
B. Handicapped people have feelings and emotions.
C. Handicapped people need to be loved and respected and *not* pitied.

D. Most handicapped people can communicate in one way or another.

E. Often, when a person loses the use of one bodily function, his other bodily functions become stronger, as blind people often have a much keener sense of hearing than people with sight.

F. Physical handicaps do not necessarily affect one's mental abilities, or vice-versa.

G. Most handicapped people have the potential to achieve.

H. Handicaps are *not* contagious.

I. Handicaps are not a punishment from God.

STRIVE NOT TO

A. It would be best not to be disappointed in your child when he stares at a handicapped person. He is probably not being malicious by doing so.

B. It would be best not to force your child into being around or conversing with handicapped people until he is ready to do so comfortably.

C. It would be best not to trivialize his fear of handicapped people. Thoughts like, "It could happen to me" are very real to a child.

D. It would be best not to fail *to answer honestly* any questions he may ask about handicaps.

Adoption

I was standing and talking with Jacqueline's parents when Jacqueline, a fourth grade girl, walked up and stood between her mom and dad. "Jacqueline sure looks a lot like each of you!" I remarked. "I know!" Jacqueline gleefully responded. "I was adopted back in the days when they matched up the babies with the parents. Nowadays, parents take what they can get!" Jacqueline's parents smiled and lovingly gave her a squeeze.

Unlike a lot of adopted children, Jacqueline knew that she

was adopted. Many adoptive parents hide the fact that their child is adopted. They say it's because the child can't handle it when, in reality, it's usually the parents who can't handle it!

Some adoptive parents fear that the natural parents will return and "run off" with the child, or that the child will grow up and want to renounce them in favor of the natural parents. If the adoptive parents have loved the child and have done an adequate job of raising him, the chances of either of these things happening are remote.

The key to handling adoption lies in the way one defines parenting. I resist assigning the term "real" parent to the parent that gives birth to the child. There is more to real parenting than conception and delivery! To me, the "real" parent is the parent that raises the child. The parent that conceives and delivers the child is the "natural" parent or the biological parent.

Having the child know who his "natural" parent is, or allowing him to meet his "natural" parent should never be a threat to the "real" parents.

A fretful adoptive parent once asked me, "But suppose Corina (her adopted girl) finds her natural parent and her natural parent begs forgiveness and wants to develop a relationship with her?" "You have nothing to fear," I said. "You are Corina's real parent and you always will be, no matter how many other relationships she develops with other people. You had the special privilege of raising her and becoming her real parent. No one can *ever* take that away from you!"

Children have a natural curiosity about their beginnings. It is extremely normal for them to have questions like, "Who are my (natural) parents?" "Where are they now?" "Why didn't they keep me?" When these questions remain unanswered, children not only suffer the consequences of unresolved questions, they begin to conjure up all kinds of terrible things in their minds. Things like, "My (natural) parents probably didn't keep me because I'm no good" or "My (adoptive) parents took me in because they felt sorry for me."

Do your adopted children a favor. Answer their questions. Let them know the truth. Honesty is the best policy. (I need to add quickly at this point that it never helps to make the natural parents "look bad." There is some good in every person and there is some good in every situation. Emphasize the good things, not the bad.)

STRIVE TO

A. Tell the truth from the very beginning about the child being adopted.
B. Answer, to the best of your ability, any questions the child may have regarding his adoption, his beginnings, his natural parents.
C. Assume the title of "real" parent if you are raising the child.
D. Assign the title of "natural" parent or "biological" parent to the parent that conceived and/or gave birth to the child.
E. Reassure the child as often as necessary that his being adopted does not mean that you love him any less than if you would have physically given birth to him.

STRIVE NOT TO

A. You need not fear having the child know who his natural parents are.
B. You need not fear the child meeting his natural parents.
C. You need not fear the natural parent returning and "running away" with the child.
D. You need not fear the child growing up and wanting to renounce you in favor of his natural parents.
E. You need not allow the child to think that the natural parent rejected him because he was "no good."

F. You need not allow the child to think that you adopted him because you felt sorry for him.

Sexual Offenses

It's a wonder that most of us ever survive childhood! Thanks to parents who cared for me and did the best they knew how in raising me, I made it through my childhood in one piece.

Some of my more traumatic experiences included the times I was sexually molested by an older man. My parents found out about the incidents and, to complicate matters, they decided to take the man to court because he refused to get professional help! If it weren't for the skillful and loving way in which my parents handled the matter, I could have really been damaged by the whole thing.

Hopefully, you will never have to deal with this trauma but, unfortunately, it is becoming more and more common. If you are ever faced with this problem, these guidelines will help you to get through it:

STRIVE TO

A. Teach the child about molestation while you are teaching him about sex. If he knows about molestation *before* he is approached, he will be aware of what's going on and may be able to avert the happening.

B. Emphasize the fact that most child-molesters are people who have not grown up sexually. Tell the child that they are in need of help and that help can only be obtained if the molester is reported.

C. Accept the child's mixed emotions about the incident. Let him know that you understand that he may have experienced "pleasurable feelings" as well as anxiety, nervousness, and guilt.

D. Maintain a relationship with the child that will allow him to come to you should he ever experience this trauma.

STRIVE NOT TO

A. It is best not to blame the child for having been molested. Remember that child-molesters have a tendency to either intimidate or persuade the child into being cooperative.
B. It is best not to allow the child to suffer guilt for having been molested. Remember that he was the *victim,* not the offender.
C. It is best not to force the child into talking about the incident over and over again. Once you have gotten the details from him so that appropriate action may be taken, drop it unless he brings it up again.
D. It is best not to discuss the situation with anyone other than those who need to be informed. Parents make it difficult for the child to "face the community" when "everyone" knows what happened.
E. You need not suspect that the child will be "prone" toward this type of activity because of his having been molested.

Summary

A. There are approximately ten traumas that seem to plague children the most. We have referred to them as "The Ten Plagues."
    1. Separation
    2. Nightmares
    3. Moving
    4. Adding a new person to the family
    5. Visits to the Doctor, Dentist and hospital
    6. Death
    7. Divorce
    8. Injuries and/or handicaps

  9. Adoption

  10. Sexual offenses

In dealing with The Ten Plagues, one should follow the "Six Steps to Coping with Trauma" in addition to taking note of the particular guidelines regarding each trauma.

13

Talking About You-Know-What

Sex Education

Nothing bothers me more than the preoccupation with sex that seems to prevail in America today. Imposing it on adults is one thing, but imposing it on children is quite another. I'm sick of having children's behavior analyzed totally in terms of their sexual needs. To listen to some people talk, one would think that the only thing children want to do all day long is masturbate, play "doctor," and peep at their naked mothers. Fathers have been instructed by some to "avoid hugging their little girls too much" and mothers have been admonished not to kiss their little boys on the mouth because these things supposedly cause children to become "sexually aroused."

All of this assumes that children see and respond to things the same way in which adults do, and this just isn't true! The sexual overtones that many adults attach to almost everything are not part of a child's thinking.

I attribute the "unacceptable" attitudes towards sex that children sometimes have—thinking that certain parts of a person's body are "nasty" or that sex in general is "dirty"—to the adults that surround them. Children are rarely allowed to see naked bodies and sex is seldom discussed in their presence. In spite of this, we expect them to believe that "the body is a beautiful creation of God" and that "sex is the most wonderful thing in the world."

One day during a discussion on "where babies come from," a sixth grade girl spoke up: "If our bodies are so beautiful, why do we always have to hide them—even at home? We don't hide other things that are beautiful!" Another girl continued, "Yeah, and if sex is so wonderful, why won't anyone ever talk about it—not even our moms and dads?" Their questions were hard for me to answer.

I believe that there is really something to the old "Forbidden Fruit" theory which says, "We want most that which we aren't allowed to have and we are intrigued most by that which we are forbidden to know."

A child who is never allowed to see a naked body will, more than likely, become sexually aroused on the few occasions that he sees one. Children who are seldom caressed or kissed on the mouth may become sexually aroused when it happens to them.

In order for sex to be "wonderful," it must be kept in perspective with all that one experiences. To avoid children becoming preoccupied with sex, I recommend that parents:

- make sex education a part of family life.
- help children to understand and accept "sex" as a marvelous part of life.
- help a child to see that his or her body is a beautiful gift from God.
- meet a child's needs for physical affection.

Making Sex Education a Part of Family Life

Part of Christopher's school schedule is a fifteen-minute "show-and-tell" time when children are allowed to bring favorite books or toys from home and show them to the class. One morning Chris's teacher was caught off-guard when one of the children brought a controversial children's book on sex to show to the class. In keeping with the rules for the show-and-tell time, the child showed three of his favorite pictures in the book. Despite the fact that Christopher and I had talked quite a lot about sex in the past, one of the pictures brought up a question in his mind that had not yet been answered.

On the way home from school, Chris told me about the book he had seen during show-and-tell. "I wondered about one of the pictures," he said, "but I wanted you to tell me about it because I knew you would tell me the right things." He then proceeded to ask if I could get the book for him so that we could talk about the picture that he did not understand.

The next day I went to the library and got the book. I went through it to prepare myself for any questions Chris might ask. The book was incredibly graphic. There were photographs of everything, including two people engaged in sexual intercourse.

I wasn't sure that I was ready for actual photographs yet, but not wanting to put Christopher off, I included the book in the stack of bedtime stories that I was going to read the children that night.

Christopher recognized the book immediately and wanted to get right into it. We began on the first page. It had pictures of a nude boy and girl approximately the same age as Chris and Lisa. We talked about the similarities and differences between the boy and girl and then made comparisons of the boy and girl in the book to Christopher and Lisa.

I could see that Christopher was getting restless. He knew "all of that stuff" and wanted to get on with it. "I'm going to turn the pages," I told them, "and if you see something you don't understand or want to talk about, stop me and we'll talk about it."

I began to turn the pages. Before long, Christopher stopped me at a page that showed another picture of a nude boy. Unlike Christopher, the boy in the picture had not been circumcised. Because he was not, the head of his penis was hidden by his foreskin. "What happened to him?" Chris asked. "Did someone cut the end of his penis off?"

We talked about circumcision and uncircumcision until I felt that Christopher understood the explanation. I had begun to turn the pages again when Christopher casually reached over, closed the book and said, "We know about all the rest. We've talked about it a lot of times. Let's get on to Bambi!"

In our family, sex is so much a normal and natural part of our conversation, that one minute we can be talking about sex and the next minute we can be talking about Bambi. We have told our children all along that there is absolutely nothing that cannot be discussed in our home. I do not agree with people who say, "There are certain subjects that should never be talked about!" Within the context of the family I believe that, as much as possible, all questions should be answered and all subjects should be discussed. Children who do not receive answers or input from their parents will draw their own conclusions (which may be wrong) or get their information from unreliable sources.

Here's an example of a young child drawing her own conclusions. In response to a picture of a bouquet of flowers, this is what she had to say:

"Hey! There's flowers like Grandma brung mommy.
Mommy had a baby!
Do you know my baby?
Mommy went to the hospital when her stomach got real big.
The doctor jumped on Mommy's stomach and the baby popped out.
Then Mommy was all better.
Can I bring my baby to school for you to see?"

Not being told about how the baby was born, she drew her own conclusions. Although they were extremely creative, they were extremely wrong.

Many fears and reservations regarding sex and childbirth come from not having the correct information. Parents have a responsibility to their child to see that his questions are answered truthfully and that the concepts he believes in are correct.

Helping Children Understand and Appreciate Sex

It is possible for parents to help children understand and appreciate sex. In order for this to happen, parents need to:

Know the subject matter. I've found that many parents do not tell their children about sex because they honestly do not know what to tell them. Often, parents need to educate themselves before they attempt to educate their child. I found the book entitled, *Everything You Always Wanted To Know About Sex, But Were Afraid to Ask,* by David Reuben, M.D. (Bantam, 1969), to be a very good book to read before I began talking to Christopher and Lisa about sex.

Begin as early as possible in a child's life. Sex education began in Christopher's life when he was two-and-a-half years old. He saw a pregnant woman in the market and asked, "Why is that lady so fat?" Many people think that an "OK" answer to that question would be, "Because she is going to have a baby." To some, this response would be sufficient because it answers the child's question without giving him unnecessary additional information.

For a long time, people have been told to "stick to the question." If a child asks a question about sex, the parents are to answer the question and say no more and no less. This is based on the assumption that if a child doesn't ask about it, he's not ready to understand it.

There are problems with totally revolving sex education around the questions that children ask. Some children do not generally ask a lot of questions, while others may not know enough to ask all the right questions. I had a father tell me of his twelve-year-old son, "I never told him about sex because he never asked." We do not wait for our children to ask when it comes to other things we think they should know about, so why do we wait for them to ask us about sex?

Instead of sitting around waiting for a child to ask questions about sex, I recommend stimulating a child's interest in it. This can be done by providing appropriate educational pictures, books, and experiences along with all the other educational tools we give our child. Given the right kind of input, a child can then ask meaningful questions and parents can respond with meaningful answers.

Stimulating a child's interest in sex at an early age makes it more likely that the parents will be the ones that are around to answer his questions. Once parents have been established in a child's mind as a valid and reliable source of information, and once the child has found that it is acceptable to talk to his parents about sex, he will continue to return to the parent whenever other questions arise—just as Christopher did with the show-and-tell book.

Some parents have asked, "How do you know when you're telling a child too much?" Let your child answer this question for you. Begin by telling your child as much of the full story as you can. He will tell you when he has had enough. He will remember what he can understand and forget what he can't understand. Each time you talk to him, he will be willing to listen to more and he will be able to understand more.

Once you've gotten the full story out, you don't have to live in fear of telling it and you don't have to fear someone else telling it in a way that is unacceptable to you. This is why I encourage parents to go as far as they can, as soon as they can. The privilege of telling a child about sex rightfully belongs to his parents. I've had some parents object to telling their child too much for fear they will go "blab it all over the neighborhood." I got around this with Christopher and Lisa by telling them, "The things that I have just told you (about sexual intercourse) are very special. They are so special that most parents want to tell their own children themselves. If you tell other children what I have told you, you will ruin it for the children and for their parents. I've appreciated being the one to tell you about sexual intercourse and I would have felt bad if someone else would have told you first. So let's let the other parents tell their own children about it and what I've told you today can be our own special secret."

Be completely honest. This includes using correct terminology. When asked where babies come from, I've had children tell me everything from "you buy them at the hospital," to "a big bird drops them down the chimney." In answer to questions regarding conception, I've heard comments like, "Mommy swallowed a seed," or "God puts an egg inside the mother and when it hatches, a baby is born."

Many of these misconceptions are manufactured by the children themselves. However, too often parents who are embarrassed to tell the truth or parents who think that children "won't understand," prefabricate the things they tell their children about sex to avoid telling the truth.

As mentioned before, misconceptions oftentimes give rise to unnecessary fears and reservations regarding sex and childbirth. In addition, they make it more difficult for a child to understand and accept the truth because, before he can learn the truth, he must *un*learn the *un*truth. If you tell the truth in the beginning, you'll never have to worry about "covering your tracks." You may not be able to tell *all* of the nitty-gritty details during your first discussion, but whatever you tell, if it's the truth, you can continue to build on it each time you talk.

As for calling the penis or vagina by anything other than their correct names, this can be detrimental, too. We call arms, *arms*, and legs, *legs*. The fact that we give nicknames to our genitals is a subtle inference that there is something "bad" about them. Although nicknames like, "peter," "wingding," "fanny," etc., are cute, they are incorrect and for this reason I recommend not using them.

Be positive. Accept and be thankful for your child's normal sex behavior.

One day, Lisa traipsed into the house and announced that she was going to be playing "doctor" outside with Christopher, Scottie, and Eric. She proceeded to gather up her equipment—which included a flashlight, blanket and stethoscope—and marched outside. Before long, I noticed four bumps underneath the blanket. Although I knew that playing "doctor" was often a part of growing up, my heart pounded. I debated whether to interfere or stand back and wait. . . . Shortly, within ten to fifteen minutes, all four children surfaced with all of their clothes on. Lisa dragged the equipment back into the house to put it away. On her way in she told me, "Mom! Guess what? Scottie and Eric have penises just like Christopher!" "Well, what did you think they would have?" I asked. "Well," she replied, "I have a vagina and Christopher is different from me, so I thought that everyone had different things!" I had told Lisa before that all girls had vaginas and that all boys had penises, but she didn't actually understand the concept until she saw it for herself.

For many children playing "doctor" is a time when they see for themselves if the concepts about sex that they have heard or conjured up are really true. If children are not made to feel guilty about engaging in sex exploration activities, they will usually explore, discover, and then be done with it for a while. Children who are forced to "sneak and hide," often become preoccupied with sex play. Many times their exploration is interrupted before their questions are answered, so they keep returning to the "doctor's office." This will continue to happen until their questions become resolved.

Masturbation is another sexual activity older children—both boys and girls—will engage in. Please do not confuse "fondling" with masturbation. Masturbation usually involves some kind of sexual climax while fondling does not.

A child may "fondle" a lock of hair or any other part of his body, including his genitals. Fondling is sometimes referred to as "playing with oneself." When a child fondles something, he usually does not concentrate on becoming sexually aroused. Instead, the enjoyment comes from feeling the texture, shape, size, etc., of the item being fondled. Fondling is often done subconsciously. Many parents are guilty of confusing fondling with masturbation. They say things like, "My child masturbates all the time!" When they are questioned further, it can be determined that the child is fondling himself rather than masturbating. Fondling is also a normal thing for children to do.

I must hasten to add at this point that becoming preoccupied with sex play or masturbation is unhealthy. By this, I mean that children who are playing doctor and/or masturbating continually, to the exclusion of all other activities, need to be helped and redirected. When sex play and masturbation become habits that control a child's life, they are no longer considered to be normal. In these cases, children usually need psychological help from a professional.

Answer any and all questions as they come up. Accept curiosity as being normal. When your child asks you questions about sex, be thankful! Every child is curious about sex, just as he is curious about other aspects of life. When children go outside the home for their sex education, they may receive it from a physiological or a biological point of view without the ethics and morality that should also go along with it.

If parents assume the responsibility of answering their child's questions, they will have the privilege of teaching sex in its proper perspective. For example, in our home, when we talk about sexual intercourse, we are careful to say that "the husband and wife" engage in the intercourse. We believe that sexual relations are a sacrament of marriage and we continually teach this to our children in subtle ways.

Another point we teach our children is that as much as

one's genitals are involved in sexual intercourse, so must one's spirit be involved. Sexual intercourse, unlike "mutual masturbation," can never be a completed process without a love relationship existing between the two people involved in it.

All of this is to say that every family has their own morals or code of ethics regarding sex. Children should not be deprived of this when receiving their sex education.

Nudity in the Home

Before I begin sharing a few things about nudity in the home, let me caution parents with adolescents. If you have never allowed your child to see your nude body, now is *not* a good time to start! Many parents, including Bruce and myself, feel that nudity is a natural part of the home atmosphere. However, I realize there are those who are uncomfortable with this and I can affirm that, too.

Nudity in the home should begin when a child is born. Nudity in the home does not mean, "parading around" in front of your children without any clothes on. Instead, it suggests that children grow up seeing male and female bodies in a natural setting at home.

When parents insist on "hiding" every time they dress or undress, children become suspicious and ask themselves, "Why don't they want me to see them? What is wrong with their bodies? Are they ashamed for me to see them?" As children experience nudity at home in a natural setting, the less likely they will want to "explore" outside the home. Children who grow up seeing the nude bodies of family members are usually not sexually stimulated by seeing them. At the same time, being able to see what a man and woman look like in real life makes sex education more understandable.

Meeting a Child's Needs for Physical Affection

Children desperately need physical affection. They need to be hugged and kissed and they need to be held and stroked. There's nothing my children love more than to have their backs lightly rubbed or their heads gently massaged.

A wise psychologist once told a friend of mine that he had better give his thirteen-year-old daughter physical affection or she would go to someone else for it.

There is nothing wrong with a display of affection between a parent and his child as long as it is consistent and as long as it is genuine. Kissing children on their lips will not sexually stimulate them if you have kissed them on the lips all of their lives. The same is true for any other kind of physical affection.

Don't allow yourself to become intimidated by other people who do not view physical affection the same way you do. Your family has the right to set its own rules. There is nothing "dirty" about loving your child and letting him know it by being physically affectionate with him.

Sex education is not a "once and for all" thing. It is indeed a continuing process. As one moves into new phases of life, he experiences different aspects of sex. Keep the lines of communication open with your child and be ready to answer his questions and give him new insights any time you are called upon to do so.

Summary

A. In order for sex to be "wonderful," it must be kept in perspective with all that one experiences. To avoid children becoming preoccupied with sex, I recommend that parents
   1. make sex education a part of family life.
   2. help children understand and accept sex as a marvelous part of life. If this is to be done, parents must
      a. know the subject matter,
      b. begin as early as possible in the child's life,

    c. be completely honest—including using correct terminology,

    d. be positive—accept and be thankful for your child's normal sex behavior, such as sex play, fondling and masturbation,

    e. answer any and all questions as they come up. Accept curiosity as normal,

3. allow nudity to be a natural part of the home atmosphere if you are comfortable with this.

4. meet the child's needs for physical affection.

14

Mommy Mows the Lawn While Daddy Washes Dishes

Sexual Identity vs. Sex Roles

"The only thing that I ever wanted for you to do was to marry a good Christian man and become a good Christian wife and mother!" my mom told me during a recent conversation. "It's not right for you to be working," she continued. "Bruce and the children need you to stay home."

These comments were typical of the "woman's-place-is-in-the-home" lectures that I—and so many other girls—had been raised on. I thought that these lectures were not affecting me until four years ago when I felt "forced" to quit my job.

Everything seemed to point to the inevitable conclusion that the time had come for me to assume my "rightful place" in the home. According to one friend, I was not "giving up" my profession, I was just "rechanneling" it—and it wouldn't be "forever," it would only be for a short period of time— sixteen to eighteen years.

Despite my friend's words of encouragement, I couldn't see how "knowing how to educate kids" related to "knowing which cleaner worked best on no-wax floors," and sixteen to eighteen years seemed like a forever! My struggle over what to do went on for some time. Finally, my fear of not being socially acceptable won over the desire to live my own life.

For six long months, I dedicated myself to fulfilling the obligations of a role that I had not chosen.

It was disastrous!

I was frustrated, hostile, resentful, and, to make matters worse, I took it out on my husband and children. Screaming rampages had become a nightly occurrence for me. One evening, in the midst of a tirade, Chris interrupted me and asked, "When are you going back to work?"

Contrary to what I had heard all of my life, the six months at home taught me that *a woman's place is where she chooses to be.* That may be in the home, and then again it may not be. This also applies to men.

When a person is allowed to *choose* which role he will assume, he does a much better job of fulfilling the demands of that role.

At this point, I feel that I need to clarify some terms because I realize that there are some areas in which a person does not have a choice. Knowing when one *can* choose and when one *cannot* choose is dependent upon knowing the difference between sexual identity and sexual roles.

Sexual Identity

A person's sexual identity is determined by:

- The person's physical characteristics—his sexual organs, facial hair, body structure, etc.
- The person's role in sexual intercourse—a man's role is to physiologically make entry, the woman's role is to physiologically receive.
- The person's role in conception—a man contributes the sperm, the woman contributes the egg.
- The person's role in the birth process—women physiologically give birth, men do not physiologically give birth.

Every child is born with a sexual identity that, generally speaking, cannot be changed. Thinking that one can change his sexual identity is not facing up to reality. Wanting to change one's sexual identity is not accepting oneself. Not facing up to reality and not accepting oneself are extremely unhealthy.

Your sexual identity is a matter over which you have no control. You were born a man or a woman with a sexual identity that cannot be changed. Part of maturing is accepting one's sexual identity.

Sexual Roles

Unlike sexual identities, sexual roles are sociological instead of physiological. A person is not born "with" a sexual role; he is born "into" it.

Sexual roles are created by society. In every society there are tasks that must be done in order to exist, function, and perpetuate itself. These tasks are divided up among the people in the society. "Roles" define which people will do which tasks. A sexual role is a role that is assigned to a person because of his or her sex. In a society that utilizes sexual roles, men are assigned specific tasks and women are assigned specific tasks. Theoretically, the tasks given to each sex are different and are designed to complement one another. An example of this is the society that assigns the food-gathering tasks to the men and the food-preparing tasks to the women.

Sexual roles are designed for the good of the society, not necessarily for the good of the individuals involved. The individuals are organized so that the society can run efficiently and effectively.

In order to make sure that every person will function within the limits of their sexual role, the society begins indoctrinating the children at a very early age. It is taught that because a person is a man or a woman, he will:

- think a certain way—men can think clearly; women cannot.
- feel a certain way—women are extremely emotional; men are not.

- act a certain way—men are stable; while women are flighty.
- like and want certain things—men like cars; women like flowers.

Some people seem to fit pretty well into their assigned roles, but there are always some individuals who simply don't fit. Those are the ones who often become socially unacceptable.

For a long time our society has struggled over what to do with the individualists who don't fit. Several alternatives to forcing people into sexual roles have been proposed, and the one that sounds the best to me suggests that while the society may define which tasks need to be done, the individuals will choose for themselves the tasks they will do.

Because Bruce and I didn't fit our sexual roles, we chose to try this alternative. Early in our marriage, we listed the tasks that needed doing and then we divided them up between ourselves. Finally, after several years of hard work, we have developed a system that seems to please everyone, including the children.

Bruce and I both work. Neither of us enjoy gardening or housework, so we have chosen to give up other things for the privilege of having a gardener and a housekeeper come once a week.

Raising the children is a job we have decided to do ourselves. I am responsible for getting the children fed, dressed, and off to school in the morning and Bruce gets them bathed and in bed at night. I am responsible for the children during the week when they are not in school; Bruce is responsible for them on the weekends when I am not there to help with them. The children have equal access to Bruce and me and they relate very well to both of us.

The children eat lunch at school; Bruce and I eat lunch at work. If I cook dinner, Bruce washes the dishes and if he cooks, I wash the dishes.

Our roles are clearly defined, but not on the basis of sex.

We have chosen for ourselves the tasks which best fit our personalities and schedules.

In addition to choosing our own tasks, we have chosen to "pool our gifts." For example, I am responsible for the aesthetic part of our home; Bruce keeps it in good repair.

I could go on about our own system, but the important point I wish to make is that being able to *choose* our tasks has made them more acceptable and enjoyable.

The Disadvantages of Forcing Sexual Roles

Several months ago, a twenty-four-year-old divorcee shared with me her reason for getting married at the age of twenty. "I didn't have any choice," she said. "I had graduated from college and it was either go back home to mom and dad or get married. You see, I had been brainwashed into believing that I couldn't make it out in the world without a man. I just couldn't face going back home, so I got married."

A short time after my talk with this woman I talked to a young man who had just left his wife. When asked why he had gotten married in the first place, he explained, "I had to! My mom had done everything for me and I didn't know how to do a thing for myself. I couldn't afford to hire a cook and housekeeper, so I married one!"

Whenever parents ask me why children should *not* be forced into a specific sexual role, I tell them that it is so that children can have the privilege of making "real" choices.

Real choices require acceptable alternatives. A choice is not a "real" choice unless there are at least two acceptable things from which to choose.

If a marriage is to work, the partners should *not* be there because they "have to be," but because they "choose to be." The choice to get married is more valid when both people have the option and the capabilities of living independently of one another.

People acquire this independence by learning both "feminine" and "masculine" skills. Every person should know how to cook, wash clothes, clean house, and darn socks. Just as they should know how to protect themselves, make minor repairs, manage their finances, and support themselves. People who are adept in all of these areas are not forced into getting married because they can't make it alone. They marry for love and for companionship—not out of necessity. Sometimes these people choose not to marry at all. At any rate, whatever they do with their life, they are doing it because they want to.

Independence that is achieved by mastering the skills of both sexual roles also strengthens a person's feeling of security. I've known so many women who fear having their husbands die or leave them, not because of love, but because they do not know how they would survive without them. I've known husbands to do the same thing. People who can make it on their own do not live in continual fear of having to live alone.

There is still another reason for not forcing children into sexual roles. Some boys are born with gifts and skills that are more suited to the feminine role, while some girls are born with gifts and skills that are more suited to the masculine role. Forcing sexual roles onto these children inhibits them from achieving their full potential. They become frustrated and often resort to misbehavior. They also react in ways that are not consistent with their real self.

Ways to Avoid Forcing Your Child into a Sexual Role

Despite the fact that Bruce and I are averse to forcing sexual roles onto children, we noticed that Christopher and Lisa were becoming slotted into their respective roles. Lisa gravitated toward things considered to be feminine and Christopher preferred the things that were defined as being masculine.

We began to take a closer look at what was happening to

our children and why. It didn't take long to uncover the subtle indoctrinations that the children were receiving, not only from the outside world, but from us as well. Without realizing it, we were encouraging our children to assume specific sexual roles by what we were doing and what we were allowing them to do.

As a result of evaluating the situation involving my own children, I was able to come up with a list of guidelines for parents who do not want to force sexual roles upon their children.

1. Model equality in your home. Assign tasks to those who want to do them or to those who do them best, regardless of their sex.
2. Encourage your child to become his or her own person, regardless of whether or not it fits into his sexual role.
3. As much as possible, control your child's environment.
   a. Purchase all kinds of toys for your children. Allow boys to have dolls and girls to have trucks.
   b. Try to make sure that the educational system of which your child is a part shares your feelings regarding sexual roles. If they do not share your feelings, at least see that they understand and respect them.
   c. Continually explain and put into perspective the input that your child receives from his environment—TV, radio, and other people.
   d. Provide non-sexist records, and books for him to hear and read.

Recently during a parent-education class, a woman spoke up. "Because of Women's Lib, I find myself being defensive about wanting to be a wife and a mother. I don't think that this is fair. My husband doesn't want me to work, nor do I want to, so why should I have to?" "You don't!" I answered. "A person's place is where he chooses to be. Women who truly desire to be wives and mothers should be allowed to stay home, just as women who want to work should be al-

lowed to work." A person functions best when he is doing
what he has chosen to do, rather than what he has been told
to do.

Summary

A. A person's sexual identity is determined by
    1. his physical characteristics.
    2. his physiological role in sexual intercourse, concep-
       tion and the birth process.
B. Good mental health and maturity are dependent upon a
   person accepting his sexual identity.
C. A person's sexual role is determined by the society of
   which he is a part and is established on the basis of tasks
   that need to be done in order to help the society exist,
   function and perpetuate itself.
D. Sexual roles are based upon the assumption that because
   a person is a man or a woman he will
    1. think a certain way,
    2. feel a certain way,
    3. act a certain way,
    4. like and want certain things.
E. People who do not fit into their sexual roles are sometimes considered to be socially "unacceptable."
F. An alternative to fitting into sexual roles is the proposal
   that suggests that, while the society may define the tasks
   that need to be done, the individuals will choose for
   themselves which tasks they will do.
G. The disadvantage of forcing sexual roles upon children is
   the fact that:
    1. sexual roles limit the choices people make.
    2. sexual roles do not encourage a person to become in-
       dependent.

    3. Sexual roles sometimes inhibit a child from using his gifts and skills to achieve his maximum potential.

H. Ways to avoid forcing your child into a sexual role are
    1. model equality in your home.
    2. encourage your child to become his or her own person.
    3. control, as much as possible, your child's environment.

I. A person functions best when he is doing what he has chosen to do, rather than what he has been told to do.

15

Let 'Em Learn the Hard Way

Socializing Children

When I was in the fifth grade, my teacher asked the class to write a story entitled, "If I Had One Wish." My story was short, simple, and to the point. It went something like this:

"If I had one wish, I'd wish that everyone in the whole world liked me the best of all. Why? Because when a person is liked, he really has all he needs."

As I grew older, I came to realize that I wasn't the only person who valued "being liked." I soon discovered that people are social beings and, as such, they have a natural desire to be liked and accepted by other people.

Being liked and being accepted is what "socialization" is all about. To be exact, *socialization is the process of integrating an individual person into a group of people.* The result of positive socialization is a person being accepted and accepting others.

Children must be socialized, not only for their own sake, but also for the sake of the people around them.

In general, there are two ways in which children can become socialized. One way is what I call, *voluntary socialization* and the other way is what I call *forced socialization.*

Voluntary Socialization

Voluntary socialization is brought about by the child that is being socialized. The process begins with the child's need to be liked and accepted. This need motivates the child to direct an action toward another person in an appeal to get that person to like and accept him. Generally speaking, the other person reacts to the child's action. If the child's action is acceptable, the other person will respond favorably toward the child. If the action is unacceptable, the other person will reject the action and possibly the child, too. Finally, the child will or will not repeat the action on the basis of whether or not it was accepted by the other person.

Charted, the Voluntary Socialization Process looks something like this.

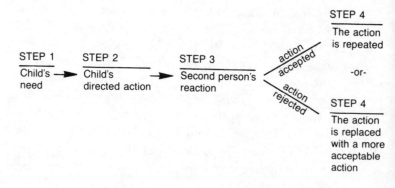

So that we can better understand voluntary socialization, here are two examples of it in action. The following observations—and the other observations that will be used in this chapter—took place in a Sunday school class consisting of approximately fifteen two-year-old children.

OBSERVATION ONE

Marcia was two years old. Her mother brought her to Sunday school for the first time. Marcia did not appear to be shy, nor did she seem to mind being left in the room by her mother.

Step 1—Marcia's need. She walked around the room, looking for something to do. She looked as though she wanted someone to play with her.

Step 2—The directed action. Marcia was carrying a small purse and, walking up to another little girl, offered it to her.

Step 3—The girl's reaction. The other girl hesitated at first, but then took the purse, opened it and dumped its contents out onto the floor.

Reaction—The action is accepted. Together, they played with the contents of the purse. When they were finished, they put the items back into the purse and set it on the table.

Step 4—The action is repeated. Marcia ran to the other side of the room, picked up a doll and ran back to the girl. She handed the doll to the girl and the girl accepted it.

OBSERVATION TWO

Kenneth was also two years old. His mother had brought him to Sunday school for the first time. Despite his vehement protests, his mother left him in the room. Kenneth withdrew. He curled up in a corner and cried during the entire "together time." Soon, free play began and he was distracted from his "separation blues" by two boys laughing and giggling on the other side of the room.

Step 1—Kenneth's need. Kenneth began to smile as he watched the boys scamper around the room. He looked as though he wanted to join into their play activities.

Step 2—The directed action. Kenneth stood up, watched the boys for a little while longer, then ran over to them and playfully pushed one of them down. Kenneth laughed.

Step 3—The boys react. The boys were stunned. The boy who had been pushed stood up and together, the two boys ran to the other side of the room, leaving Kenneth behind.

Reaction—The action is rejected.

Step 4—The action is not repeated. Kenneth became solemn again, ran back to his chair, sat down and began sucking his thumb.

As evidenced by both observations, voluntary socialization is a process that is based upon "trial and error." A child wanting to be accepted directs an action toward another child. If the action gains the desired response, the child will have a tendency to repeat the action, or do something similar to it again. If the action does not gain the desired response, the child will, more than likely, abandon the action. (Often, an action may have to be rejected several times before the child gets the message that it is unacceptable.)

Marcia's initial action—that of offering her purse to the other little girl, led to her being accepted and thus, she ventured a second action which was to offer the girl a doll. These two experiences served as a reinforcement to Marcia that "sharing" is a good way to gain acceptance.

When Kenneth pushed the boy down, his action was immediately rejected. Thus, he learned the hard way that "pushing" is not the way to say, "Let's be friends!"

As it did for Kenneth, the voluntary socialization process often involves learning the hard way. Although learning the hard way—by making mistakes—is often painful, it is one of the most effective ways to learn because children not only learn *how* to act, but they learn *why* they should act a certain way.

Allowing children to socialize themselves by the voluntary socialization process has several advantages. To begin with, this process can take place with or without adults being present. This means that whenever and wherever there are two or more children present, socialization can take place. Children who socialize themselves learn to solve social problems on their own. They do not rely on adults to solve their problems for them. This usually results in less "tattling." In addition to this, children learn to assume the responsibility for their own actions. They do not get in the habit of blaming their parents or anyone else for their mistakes.

Because of its "hit or miss" approach (sometimes it takes many "misses" before there is a "hit") the voluntary approach to socialization takes a little longer. However, because it involves self-directed learning, its effects are longer lasting.

Most adults would agree that it is best for children to socialize themselves, but too often they become anxious because the process isn't working fast enough or because they can't stand to see children make a mistake. Their over-anxiousness and impatience often result in interfering with the voluntary socialization process and hinders its completion.

The following two observations are examples of what I mean.

Observation Three

Paul was two-and-a-half years old. For two years, he had been attending Sunday school at the church where the observation took place. Paul's father accompanied him to the classroom. As soon as Paul was in the room, he spotted Tim meticulously building an exceptionally high tower with the blocks.

Step 1—Paul's need. Paul became excited. He looked as though he wanted to play with the blocks, too.

Step 2—The directed action. While his father talked to the teacher, Paul ran over to Tim's tower and gleefully knocked it down.

Step 3—Tim's reaction. Tim became very angry and started toward Paul as though he was going to hit him. Paul let out a shriek and began to run away.

Reaction—Paul's action is rejected.

Intervention—His father and the teacher turned around just in time to see Tim chasing Paul around the room with a clenched fist. They rushed to Paul's aid. The teacher held on to Tim while Paul clung onto his father's leg. "We mustn't hit," the teacher said. "Paul wants to play with the blocks, too, and you must learn to share."

Tim was coaxed into apologizing to Paul and Paul returned to play with the blocks while Tim was confined to the "thinking chair." *The process is incomplete.*

Paul's action in knocking Tim's blocks down was unacceptable and Tim was about to show him why when the adults intervened. Their intervention not only hindered Paul from learning a valuable lesson, it reinforced several misconceptions, such as:

- Screaming is the way to get adults to notice me and come to my rescue. (Without realizing it, adults actually encourage whining and crying by rewarding it with attention.)
- I can get away with things that adults do not see.

OBSERVATION FOUR

Nan was two-and-a-half years old. While her mother was talking to the teacher, she entered the room. She had brought a small toy with her to Sunday school. Sarah spotted the toy that Nan was holding and ran over to her and asked to see it.

Step 1—Nan's need. Nan seemed to like Sarah and wanted to play with her, but was hesitant about sharing her toy.

Step 2—The directed action. Nan tried to redirect Sarah's attention to an abandoned wheel toy in the middle of the room. "You sit, I'll push," Nan said.

Step 3—Sarah's response. Sarah could not be distracted

from Nan's toy. She grabbed at it, but Nan managed to keep it out of her reach.

Nan's action is rejected. Frustrated, Sarah screamed, "I hate you!"

Intervention. At this point, Nan's mother ran over to her and took the toy from her. "You must learn to share!" she said as she gave the toy to Sarah.

Nan flew into a rage and began throwing a tantrum. Finally, Nan's mother took her out of the room, leaving Sarah to play with Nan's toy. *The process is incomplete.*

If we were to chart these two observations, they would look something like this:

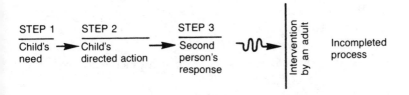

In both situations, adults, trying to do the right thing, hindered more than they helped by not allowing the children the privilege of solving their own problems.

If children are to solve their own problems and socialize themselves, certain guidelines must be followed by the adults that surround them. They are:

1. Discourage "tattling" by not responding to it unless someone's life or property is in danger.
2. As much as possible, allow children to settle their own disagreements. Do not allow them to pull you into their

arguments. Tell them, "Your problem is between you two people. It has nothing to do with me and, therefore, I refuse to get involved. You will have to settle the problem on your own."

3. Encourage children to settle their problems with "words" rather than with physical abuse. Teach them that if their words don't work, they must learn to "walk away."

4. Intervene in a disagreement only when a child is being severely abused physically or emotionally. On the *few* occasions that you must intervene,

   a. do not make any judgments without knowing both sides.

   b. do not take sides.

   c. work through the situation with both children so that they can learn how to better solve the problem the next time they are faced with it.

5. If children insist on bickering and fighting, do not stop them. Remember, however, that they do *not* have the right to impose their bickering and fighting on you. Insist that they do it in a manner or a place where you will not have to listen to it.

6. When children have agreed to settle their disagreements one way, do not "jump in" and try to reverse their decision if you happen to think it is wrong. Instead, let them find out for themselves whether or not their decision was wrong.

Forced Socialization

The forced socialization process usually begins with a combination of the parent's need to be accepted and recognized as a "good parent" and the child's need to be socialized. The parent motivates (or forces) a child to direct an action towards another person. The child directs the action as requested and the other person usually accepts it. Further reinforcement comes when the parent affirms the child.

Charted, the forced socialization process looks like this:

STEP 1	STEP 2	STEP 3	STEP 4	STEP 5
Parent's need, plus the child's need	Parent motivates the child to direct an action	Child's directed action	Second person's acceptance and parent's affirmation	The action is repeated (only when the parent is present)

A few examples of forced socialization are children who are
- made to say "please," "thank you," "excuse me," "I'm sorry," without realizing or meaning what they say.
- forced to "show respect" for someone they do not really respect.
- made to share when they don't really want to share.
- forced into acting a certain way when they don't understand or agree with the reason for which they are doing it.

Parents who prefer this approach to socializing children usually do so because it allows them to be in control. Often times, they fear having their child make mistakes so they try to control his life in order to prevent him from making the mistakes that they made when they were children.

In addition to this, forced socialization is easier and faster than voluntary socialization. Telling a child to "do it because I told you to" takes less time and effort than giving him a long, involved explanation or allowing him to discover for himself why he should or should not do something.

Unlike children who are socialized via the voluntary process, children who are socialized by forced socialization function in a "socially acceptable" way to avoid being punished or to gain approval from their parents.

Often times, these children revert to socially unacceptable behavior when their parents are not around because the threat of punishment is gone or because no one is around to affirm them for being good. Forced socialization may be faster and easier, but I feel that voluntary socialization brings about more meaningful and longer-lasting results. For this reason, I recommend that children socialize themselves.

Summary

A. People are social beings and, as such, they have a natural desire to be liked and accepted by other people.

B. Children must be socialized—not only for their sake, but for the sake of the people around them.

C. In general, there are two ways that children can be socialized: Voluntary socialization and Forced socialization.

D. Voluntary socialization
   1. is brought about by the child's need to be liked and accepted.
   2. involves four steps:
      a. the child's need,
      b. the child's directed action,
      c. the second person's reaction—either an acceptance or a rejection of the child's directed action,
      d. the action is either repeated or replaced by the child.
   3. is based on trial and error.
   4. involves learning the hard way—by making mistakes. The advantages to having children socialize themselves are:
      a. In addition to learning *how* they should act, they learn *why* they should act a certain way.
      b. The process can take place with or without adults being present.
      c. Children learn to solve their own problems. They do not rely on adults to do it for them.

d. Children learn to assume the responsibility for their own actions. They do not get into the habit of blaming others.

e. The results are more meaningful and longer lasting.

Most adults would agree that it is best for children to socialize themselves via the voluntary socialization process. However, they become anxious because they can't stand to see children make mistakes. This causes them to interfere in the process and hinder it from completing itself.

E. In order for the voluntary socialization process to be effective, parents must avoid becoming involved in the process.

F. Forced socialization

1. begins with a combination of the parent's need to be accepted and recognized as a "good parent" and the child's need to be socialized.

2. involves five steps:

a. parent's need, plus child's need,

b. parent motivates or forces the child to direct an action,

c. child directs the action,

d. second person accepts action and parent affirms child,

e. the action is repeated (only when the parent is present).

G. Reasons why parents choose the forced socialization approach:

1. Parents are in control.

2. The parents can make sure that their child never makes a mistake.

3. The process is easier and faster than the voluntary process.

Ending

Unlike "Fairy Tale happy endings" that come about with little or no effort, happy endings in real life take real work. In this book, I have attempted to outline basically what is required to make a happy ending possible.

I realize that, to some, it may seem overwhelming, but the trick to successful parenting is taking one step at a time.

I suggest beginning by really believing in yourself and then believing in your child. Once you have taken these two steps, the rest will begin to fall into place and you *and* your child will be on your way to living HAPPILY EVER AFTER.